OLD LIVERPOOL

UNIFORM WITH THIS BOOK

*

OLD COTSWOLD
by Edith Brill

OLD DEVON
by W. G. Hoskins

OLD DORSET
by M. B. Weinstock

OLD MENDIP
by Robin Atthill

OLD NOTTINGHAM
by Malcolm I. Thomis

OLD SOUTHAMPTON SHORES
by J. P. M. Pannell

OLD LIVERPOOL

ERIC MIDWINTER MA DPhil

DAVID & CHARLES : NEWTON ABBOT

ISBN 0 7153 5335 7

For Daniel

Set in 11 pt Garamond, 1 pt leaded
and printed in Great Britain by
Latimer Trend and Company Limited, Plymouth
for David & Charles (Publishers) Limited
South Devon House Newton Abbot Devon

Contents

Chapter		Page
	List of Illustrations	7
	Introduction	11
1.	The Theatre Royal and after	23
2.	The first Grand National	40
3.	The inauguration of the Liverpool Police Force	55
4.	Liverpool and the new Poor Law	67
5.	The cholera and Doctor Duncan	85
6.	The struggle for water and drains	100
7.	The early years of the Liverpool School Board	115
8.	Everton Football Club: the opening seasons	131
9.	The retail revolution: David Lewis and Owen Owen	149
10.	The fame of Florence Maybrick	161
11.	The sectarian troubles and the Police Inquiry of 1909–10	172
	Bibliography	188
	Acknowledgements	193
	Index	195

List of Illustrations

PLATES | *Page*

Old Liverpool 17

Liverpool 18

The Theatre Royal, until recently a cold-storage depot, and the nearby Playhouse Theatre, with its brand-new restaurant 35

The famous Empire Theatre, one of Liverpool's only two remaining commercial theatres 36

The 1839 Grand National—the first year the title was used 53

The start of the 1966 Grand National 53

Michael James Whitty, first Chief Constable of Liverpool 54

Walton Prison, opened 120 years ago and still in full use 54

The Liverpool Poor House, about 1770 71

The latest old people's homes, Leighton Dene, Liverpool 72

The second Liverpool Infirmary on Brownlow Hill, 1828 89

Doctor Duncan 89

The interior of a Victorian wash-house in Liverpool 90

Christopher Bushell, first chairman of the Liverpool School Board 90

Chatsworth Primary School, one of Liverpool's first Board Schools, still active today 107

Everton Football Club, 1883–4 108

Everton Football Club, today 125

Lewis & Co. in its earliest days 126

Owen Owen now 143

Florence Maybrick 144

George Wise 144

LINE DRAWING IN TEXT

Part of Benson's Plan of Liverpool 8, 9

Part of Benson's Plan of Liverpool

Introduction

The history of Merseyside is greater in quality and significance than that of many a nation. To speak of 'local' history with reference to the slave trade, the Liverpool–Manchester railway, the establishment of the port, the Irish immigrations, Gladstone, the development of public health, and a dozen other facets of Liverpool's story, seems odd, for Liverpool has reflected, more especially since the eighteenth century, not only the national but the international picture, and it is such that it is especially important to the local historian. Local history that is inward-looking and engrossed in its own context has a pleasing interest, but if it is to rise above the merely antiquarian, it must act as a governor on the broader situation and must seek to illumine the whole by an intensification of focus on the part.

This is not intended as a formal history of Liverpool, either generally or over the last century or so. Indeed, it would be simpler to write the history of a country like Norway or Portugal, for no one has yet succeeded in producing a definitive work on this bubbling, fluid, dynamic city. This is no more than a set of brief sketches that hint like a series of quickly pencilled cartoons, at the profundity beyond. They form an anthology of selected essays on aspects of Liverpool life and society culled mainly from the last one hundred and fifty years.

They have four characteristics. First, they avoid the well-known and well-rehearsed. The docks, the railway, the slave trade, the shipping, the Irish have been avoided or simply referred to obliquely, and an attempt has been made to examine less famous events and persons, without, it is hoped, descending too near the level of matters which are obscure because they are humdrum and tedious. Second, their motley assortment is dictated by personal pique and choice. Certain similarities are apparent—a fascination by sport and the theatre couples with a more serious obsession with the major social problems of poverty, disease, crime, and ignorance. Some claim for a wide range might be pressed. The rule is run over cholera and the Grand National, over Mrs Maybrick and sectarian strife. Third, they practically all had repercussions outside Liverpool; Dr Duncan was the first Medical Officer of Health in England, not only in Liverpool; Everton FC created a national as well as a Liverpolitan image; David Lewis was instrumental in assisting a retail reconstruction of far-reaching proportions, and so on. Fourth, almost all of them contribute in some fashion to the present life of the city.

This last is probably the most important point. When history is merely about the past, it can become moribund, and it lives only when it illuminates the present and makes it more comprehensible. Each cameo treated here survives. Sometimes this is a purely architectural survival, like the old Theatre Royal, which became a cold storage depot. Sometimes it is still physical and tangible, like the public health or schools systems begun in the nineteenth century. Sometimes it lies in the city's psyche or culture, and the Maybrick legend or the Orange and Green factions are examples of this kind of survival. Sometimes it is a reflection of the day-to-day life of Merseyside in such elements as football, or the department store that is a household name. Whether of the flesh or the spirit of Liverpool, this is a highly selective survey of a few of the roots and origins of its present condition.

A county as well as a national perspective becomes apparent. Liverpool is rightly thought of as a highly idiosyncratic and individualistic city. Beyond that it is seen as cosmopolitan, with a deep Irish influence, and, what is less well exhibited but equally valuable, with an interesting Welsh element. It is too easily forgotten that Liverpool is a Lancashire town, and that both its history and geography are solidly linked with the County Palatine. Manchester is more clearly seen as a Lancashire city, but the commercial weight of Liverpool has chiefly rested on its Lancastrian hinterland. Many of the elements of Liverpool life represented here demonstrate this Lancastrian flavour—football, theatre, the retail trade, the Grand National, the relatively high proportion of Roman Catholics in the North West, water supply, and so forth.

Thus even a brief and cursory résumé of some aspects of Liverpool over the last century or so may become a glance through a lens that reveals glimmerings of regional, national, and world history. Above all, Old Liverpool anticipates the present; it is not a nostalgic retrospect. The city which prides itself on its brash new motto, 'the city of change and progress', would not thank anyone for a review of antiquities.

The city of Liverpool is, then, a splendid frame for these brief excursions into its past, an interesting frame and one that needs closer delineation if this ad hoc selection of items is to enjoy the benefits of interconnection. Liverpool had a late start and a slow one. It was bypassed by the Romans and ignored by the Domesday commissioners; the Romans preferred Wigan and the Domesday Book refers curtly to the West Derby hundred without any mention of Liverpool; the anglo-saxon ring of Bootle and the Norse town of Skelmersdale appear to predate Liverpool. It is as though Liverpool has been attempting to revenge these humiliations ever since. The name itself has no romance, no ornithological nor mythical tales of liver birds to excite the imagination. 'Liverpool' is English, twelfth-century and realistic—the liver-coloured, dingy or muddy pool. The cap still fits.

As Liverpool proceeds to circle itself today with new towns and development areas, it is appropriate to recall its own origin as a medieval 'new town' in 1207 under letters patent issued by King John. Hitherto Liverpool had been of little note, no more than some farmland on the slopes where Islington and London run, with a little settlement nearer the water. The Norman castle of West Derby stood over to the south east, with the forest 'chases' of Toxteth and Croxteth severely protected for royal use. John was keen to develop a new port in the North West, possibly to counteract the influence of Chester. He urged his subjects to take up 'burgages' in Liverpool and to establish a new community under his patronage and with all the advantages of being a royal borough.

These pioneer Liverpolitans settled down in the spur of land formed by the Mersey and the Pool. The Pool, in actuality, was a small, broad-necked offshoot of the Mersey, flowing through and emerging in what now is the Whitechapel–Canning Place area. It was the Pool which was Liverpool's first harbour and the basis of its trading prosperity. These new burgesses thus, in effect, colonised Liverpool, each with his burgage or plot of land and, like his later wild-west equivalent, a wooden shack. Seven streets were laid to the east of the Pool, seven streets which still throb at the heart of Liverpool's commercial activity. They were Castle Street, High Street, and Oldhall Street, running parallel to the Mersey along a slight hump or ridge and with Water Street, Dale Street, Chapel Street, and Tithebarn Street, making right angles with them. Overshadowed by Chester and with perhaps no more than a dozen ships safe in the deep anchorage of the Pool, Liverpool remained unchanged for four centuries, and the royal borough saw few alterations until the last half of the seventeenth century. The next three hundred years were to be as dynamic as the previous four hundred has been static. The huge expansion of overseas trade was to transform the peaceful medieval creek into a teeming, international port. Topographically, the hub of this development was to be the seafront and its seven seminal streets. In the initial stages of this evolution, as well as the commercial and domestic extension, the Pool disappeared and by the eighteenth century new harbours were being built on the river bank. Bounded by the Mersey estuary to the west and with its southern expansion soon to be blocked by the river cutting eastward from the estuary, Liverpool was forced to look, as it were, over its shoulder into the Lancashire hinterland for room to expand.

Liverpool classically depicts the urban cycle of growth and decay. Fastened in by the angle formed by estuary and river, its outward growth has been more rhythmic and simpler to observe than many a more centrally located city. Each heave forward economically has set up a series of pulsations which drew more and more of Lancashire under the sway of Liverpool, and as this has happened, so has each sector of Liverpool undergone the full gamut of social change. Consider the gradual construction of the docks as the catalyst for this urban development: by 1715 the Old Dock had replaced the Pool and, by the end of the century, four other docks were added to give Liverpool England's best dockland provision; two more were added in 1825 and then, in a whirlwind progression, the newly formed Dock Committee constructed no fewer than twenty-two docks in a little over thirty years, principally under the control of that abrasive engineer, Jesse Hartley. After 1857 the Mersey Docks and Harbour Board took up the cudgels. A dozen more docks were built, pushing now into Birkenhead and Bootle and culminating in the massive Gladstone Dock, opened in 1927. Now, to the north of the Gladstone Dock, an even larger dock is under construction. In 1660 perhaps little more than a thousand people lived in Liverpool. Today there are nearly three-quarters of a million. Such has been the effect of overseas trade since the Restoration.

This combine of commercial expansion and population caused, of course, reverberation upon reverberation. As the business and trading sections grew, the dockers and other workers were pushed out, and in turn the merchant and professional classes were dislodged and began to gobble up the peripheral country-side, a process helped by the advance of transport, again the necessary adjunct both of growing trade and a growing populace. In 1726 Liverpool's first turnpike road was begun in order to link the borough with Prescot and, during the eighteenth century, several 'navigations' and 'cuts' were completed, including the be-ginning of the Liverpool–Leeds canal. In 1830 the Liverpool–Manchester railway ushered in the bewildering mosaic of Mersey-side railways. Slowly the transport media evolved, and where once a coach from Water Street reached London in thirty hours at best, the electric train can now manage the journey in some-thing over two hours. Steam came to the river, to the canals, and to the sea. Soon the electric trams, 'the green goddesses' of scouse lore, the buses, and the private cars helped speed travellers back and to.

To the north, development followed the coastline. Bootle, where Gladstone saw wild roses grow in the village centre, was in quick succession rural retreat, merchant suburb, artisan quarter, and dockland. As the docks pushed north, the middle classes followed the suburban railway through Crosby to Southport. Similarly in the south; aided by the ferry boats and the Mersey Tunnel, the migration to the Wirral commenced and has yet to end, as more and more people gather, like so many Jacobites, 'over the water'. Like movements occurred in the central areas. Walking from Pierhead or Lime Street away from the city centre, one is quickly aware of the radial spokes shooting outwards to-ward Preston, Manchester, Warrington and so on. The gradient of the ascent is surprising. Compared with the usually dull flatness of West Lancashire, the climb out of Liverpool is quite steep, as the city stubs of these radial roadways—Brownlow Hill, Mount Pleasant, Mount Vernon, Edge Hill, Everton Brow—reveal. From the imposing vantage-point of Everton Heights and with the view assisted by the demolition of great tracts of housing, one can survey a vast industrial landscape from above, right down to the estuary and the docks and across to the Wirral and the Welsh mountains beyond.

By dint of these processes, Liverpool has come to represent a rough half-circle bounded by water and dissected by rail and road links to the hinterland. The railway lines from Lime Street Station (opened in 1836) also indicate the sloping character of the city as they negotiate their way through the sidings and tunnel works which had to be laboriously dug through Liverpool's hilly surround. The half-wheel can also be approximately divided into a series of arcs or swathes, curving around from north to south. At the hub lies the business and mercantile world, pivoting on the Pierhead, dominated by the Royal Liver Buildings, the Dock Board offices and the Cunard headquarters. Somewhere about the line of Lime Street and the Adelphi Hotel this business and shopping world begins imperceptibly to merge into the inner area of downtown Liverpool. This is a grey, transitional region of decaying merchant properties, worn-out artisan terraces, planner's blight and highrise redevelopment. It describes a curving band from Kirkdale and Scotland Road in the north, via Everton, Kensington and Granby around to Toxteth and Harrington in the south, with both ends just touching the Mersey. Beyond the 'dead heart' of the city, through an overlapping twilight zone of traditional working-class houses, there lies another semicircle, the suburban belt. It follows the line of Liverpool's ring road, Queen's Drive, whose eight or so miles follow an arc from Bootle around to Aigburth. It is also marked by the impressive, almost interlocking loop of parks that swing through Liverpool's suburban range. It was in the mid-nineteenth century that the Liverpool authorities properly insisted on preserving this feature as housing spread rapidly, and thus Walton, Wavertree, Sheil, Stanley, Newsham, Sefton, and Prince's Parks continue to avoid the pressures of building and remain an unusually undisturbed and attractive feature. The suburbs, of course, do not stop at the city boundary, and the whole Merseyside conurbation needs must be drawn into the perspective. Naturally, this tale of the evergrowing semicircle is a drastic simplification, but it suggests a useful outline for those to whom Liverpool's format is strange.

This cyclic decay and renewal, coupled with the cramping limitations of sea and river, have produced several fascinating and

Page 17   Old Liverpool

Page 18
Liverpool

illuminating elements. Nor is the cycle ended; the new docks, the string of new towns and redevelopment points—Kirkby, Skelmersdale, Runcorn, Cantril Farm, Speke, Netherleigh—on the edges of the major conurbation, a new tunnel and massive new roadworks; these remind us that the booming times of progress, with their subsequent jarring dislocations, are not over for Liverpool. It is odd to stand in one or another place in Liverpool and remember the history that has washed over it. Prince Rupert camped on Everton Brow (a pub name commemorates his visit) and set up his artillery to bombard the little borough on the line of Lime Street and St George's Hall; the once majestic façade of Upper Parliament Street has unhappily degenerated into overcrowded, multi-let apartments; David Lewis walked from his home in Prince's Park to the store each morning. That too is now in a sorry and impoverished area.

But the magnetism of the city centre and, more realistically, its unavoidability are maintained. People live on the very doorsteps of commerce; empirically, one might hazard the guess that more children are visible in the centre of Liverpool than most other comparable cities. They seem to swarm over St George's Plateau, the Wellington Monument across from the library, museum and art gallery in William Brown Street, as well, as might be expected, over the tempting purlieus of the Pierhead and the huge new bus depot. Certainly municipal housing begins close to the city centre and certainly Liverpool has the highest proportion of retail trade in its centre of all towns in the United Kingdom. So much of the population automatically turns seaward to the city for its shopping, whether to the fine department stores, of which Lewis's and Owen Owen still remain as important as any, or to the several markets, like Paddy's market or St John's Market, where the saltiness of Liverpool life may be tasted at its most astringent. The centre manages none the less to retain a medieval flavour here and there, with the incredibly narrow and mysterious set of crowded byways near Exchange Station with names like Leather Lane and Hackins Hey. Nearby and pushing with elegant assurance from out the normal line of Water Street is the town hall, normally accepted, particularly internally, as one of Europe's finest examples of eighteenth-century architecture and decor. And over the road in complete contrast, is drab, old James Street Station, which has lately received a well-earned face-lift and is claimed to be England's oldest passenger station. In Sir Thomas Street stand the old School Board offices, a typically gaunt and black Victorian structure, now housing its successor, the Liverpool Education Committee. Mainly under its jurisdiction, the city boasts literally hundreds of schools, many of striking quality, either educationally or physically. There is the squat, square blackness of the Liverpool Collegiate on Shaw Street. There is North Corporation Street School, near Scotland Road, England's oldest surviving municipal school. There are splendid samples of 1870s School Board architecture, like Chatsworth Street or Queens Road Schools. There are excellent new educational premises like the College of Building, the Liverpool Polytechnic, and the University.

Downtown Liverpool has unpredictable and unusual pleasures for the wanderer. As great parts of it once housed the upper and middle classes, there is a kind of cultural debris left after their evacuation to Southport, Ormskirk, and the Wirral. Ironically, much of Liverpool's purported culture resides in what is classified as a socially deprived area. The University, its campus ever widening, and the Philharmonic Hall, are located there. Many of the city's hospitals—each grim outline a tribute to its Victorian founding fathers—are solidly present in the inner city ring. Rodney Street, just off Mount Pleasant, is an interesting case. It has taken Rudyard Kipling's advice in 'If' and kept its head when all around others are losing theirs. It is called 'Liverpool's Harley Street'; its houses are beautifully maintained and very expensive, often complete with ornamental Victorian boot-scrapers. Gladstone was born down Rodney Street, the Cloughs lived there, and Dr Duncan first practised down there. There are several splendidly ornate public houses near by like the Philarmonic Hotel, the Grapes Hotel and the Prince of Wales Hotel. They are huge, brown-flavoured, leathery establishments with cavernous lavatories and lots of Victoriana. Several old streets repay detailed attention. Chatham Street with its rare Victorian pillarbox, Soho Street, with its old coachworks, Granby Street, with its exotic immigrant flavour, and so on.

The churches, numbered in their scores, are sometimes interesting for their changed usage. One in Chatham Street is an audio-visual centre for the University; another near Great George's Place, hard by the intriguing Chinese quarter, is an arts centre. By a legal quirk of circumstances, Prince's Avenue boasts umpteen churches (including a Methodist church with Arthur Dooley's West Indian 'Christ' on its wall and a church taken over for Chinese worship) but not one pub. Overall, and still in this downtown area, the two cathedrals gaze at one another down Hope Street. They are quite close enough to compare at a glance. A commentator has said, in the anthropomorphic way that architectural observers have, that the Anglican cathedral, very nearly the largest in Europe, dominant and assured in its mock-Gothic squareness, exudes the brash confidence of the Edwardian world; whereas the modernistic, nervy spikeyness of the Roman Catholic cathedral catches the doubts and anxious hopes of mid-twentieth century man. The former is still not completed after more than half a century; the latter was constructed in a few short years. Visit the one for its pride and grandeur and for its memorials to persons like William Huskisson and Kitty Wilkinson; go to the other for its stark, simple, no-nonsense impact. Needless to say, the irreverent Liverpolitan soon nicknamed the Metropolitan Cathedral either 'the Mersey Funnel' or 'Paddy's Wigwam'.

Over to the north are the football grounds. It is odd that in a city which is if anything self-conscious about its religious and footballing divisiveness, the major agencies are adjacent to one another, and just as the cathedrals stare at each other, so the football grounds, Anfield and Goodison Park, are scarcely half a mile apart. They seem to grow out of the endless rows of terraced houses, outside which on Saturday afternoons the youngsters ply their parking trade with much aplomb and skill. Several writers have, without becoming too fanciful, drawn analogies between cathedral and football ground. With so many tiny houses clustered around their high walls, they do take on something of the ambience of the tribal shrine. The fierce identification, the chants and counter-chants, the songs and psalms of praise, the hero-worship and the adulation, the floodlight towers spiralling high above—these all contribute to this atmosphere. It is a serious business. Many a school must avoid red, blue, orange, or green when choosing its sports colours.

Beyond this downtown belt, this curious mélange of the drab and the colourful, the suburbs begin. They are, of course, relatively new. One must recall that Crown Street was in 1835, at the time of the Municipal Reform Act, the town's eastern boundary, with green fields a few yards beyond. Now Crown Street stands at the centre of devastation and demolition, indicative of the speed at which the cycle moves. The suburbs seem to blur together somewhat, but here and there one finds a spark of the village community which most of them were until well on into the last century. Some of them like Allerton, Woolton, Garston, Aigburth, Croxteth, West Derby, or Kirkdale, might claim to be older communities than Liverpool itself. Several of them jealously preserved their independence and retained some autonomy until near the end of the nineteenth century; for instance, Garston, Woolton, Wavertree and others had their own local boards of health while West Derby and Toxteth both organised their own Poor Law unions. Gradually they were assimilated, partly because the large-scale services, like transport, sanitation, and water-supply, dictated the administrative good sense of amalgamation. There is still a tang of the independent township about some of these areas.

Liverpool, then, has this approximate sandwiching of three or four curved layers, with its natural proclivity to press down to the sea and with a number of major radials leading across the layers. It is easy to walk about. The splendour of docks and cathedrals and public buildings is not difficult to discover. But probably it is the eccentricities and oddities, filling in the crevices and gaps among these stately institutions, that give real life to the city. It is not a simple matter to produce a guidebook about Liverpool. Possibly it is preferable to wander regardless, looking and listening haphazardly and finding unpredictable rewards. It is because of this varied and wide-ranging character that one must finally re-emphasise that this book does no more than pick several of the growth-points of Liverpool life and attempt to describe them.

CHAPTER ONE

The Theatre Royal and after

The week this was written the Royal Court Theatre, last but one of Liverpool's commercial theatres, sadly closed with a Brian Rix farce and turned for succour to the blandishments of bingo. It had been opened in 1881, replacing the Amphitheatre, Great Charlotte Street, which had been active since 1825. The Royal Court had housed many famous touring plays and opera and ballet companies, as well as offering accommodation to the more high-powered local societies. Now it slotted, if only temporarily, into that long, dismal tale of theatre closures which, since soon after the war, has developed another series, this time of cinema closures.

Although its media might change, entertainment itself still mightily persists, with the television and recording companies in the van. In the sixties, Liverpool, with the Beatles its prime representatives, looked to become the home of popular culture, and a subsidiary industry was erected to analyse and dissect the energetic phenomenon of the Mersey Beat in sociological and psychological terms. Whatever the contemporary explanation, there was no denying the rich tradition of popular entertainment in Liverpool. It is usually suggested that this evolved around the crowded, cosmopolitan character of the town. A port draws people together from the world over, and Liverpool has a curious amalgam of Lancastrian, Irish, and Welsh, alongside a dozen other ethnic groups. A port is rarely over-bountiful, and social crises, small and large, have doubtless honed the edges of Liverpool's cosmopoly. F. J. Turner, the famous American historian and inventor of the concept of 'the vanishing frontier' with reference to the growth of the United States, described a similar if much larger melting-pot across the Atlantic. As phases of

23

colonial development succeeded one another, each imparting its own shock and impact, the atypical cultural manifestations were, according to Turner, 'vital entertainers', among whom he might include many from Mark Twain to Bob Hope. The Beatles and their kind are 'vital entertainers', and they are the professional top skimmed from the throbbing zest and acuteness of a busy, maritime city. Before them Liverpool was well known as a breeding-ground for stand-up comics, of whom Robb Wilton, Tommy Handley, Arthur Askey, Ted Ray, and Ken Dodd are gifted examples.

The tradition may be stretched, and with stretching, it must be confessed, thinning, to medieval times and the mummers and players connected with the church. Juggler Street, it is argued, is derived from *jongleur*, a travelling entertainer of the late medieval period, and it is thought plays were shown in Water Street in Tudor times. In 1571 the Corporation 'agree that no players of interludes, jugglers, gesters, or wandering people bryngyng into this towne any monstrous or strange beasts, or other visions voyde or vayne, to theyre lucre and distresse of the qns. subjects without License of Mr. Maior tyme beyng'. A little later 'the wanderers with the hobby horse' were placed in the stocks, an early insight into the Liverpolitans' reputation as a critical audience.

The Earl of Leicester's Company played, it is thought, at Lathom House and Knowsley Hall, touring the stately homes of England after the fashion of the day. Shakespeare was, of course, a member of Leicester's troupe, and it is an amiable speculation that he may have tasted the tang of Liverpool life, possibly lending an ear for snippets of dialogue for his 'rude mechanicals'. Even stronger was the belief that William, sixth Earl of Derby, might challenge Francis Bacon as the hypothetical writer of Shakespeare's plays. It is reported that he was ever 'busye in pennyng commodyes for the commoun players'. More certainly Shakespeare's nephew Charles Hart, the actor and Nell Gwynne's first lover, was known in Liverpool, and he attended Prince Rupert at the Siege of Liverpool in 1644 during the Civil War. And the Cockpit Yard Theatre in Moor Street was probably Liverpool's first exclusively theatrical establishment, dating from about the same time.

The major theme of Liverpool's theatrical history, however, was to be the story of the Theatre Royal. In 1768 Mr Gibson of the Drury Lane Theatre, which stood where Brunswick Street now runs, agitated for a Theatre Royal in Liverpool. It was not a fanciful title. A Theatre Royal was constructed and operated under Royal Letters Patent, and these enabled it to perform plays under important legal privileges and regulations. The House of Lords at first rejected the request, but then relented, and in 1771 Gibson was granted Letters Patent for twenty-one years, 'to form, entertain, govern, privilege and keep a company of comedians for his majesty's service in the town of Liverpool'.

Williamson Square was chosen as the site, and at that time it was still countrified, what is now Whitechapel being a piece of swampy marsh. £6,000 in £200 shares was raised in an hour, and the new theatre was to displace Gibson's old haunt, the Drury Lane. Unluckily, Gibson himself died within weeks of the receipt of the patent, and his mistress Mrs Bennett inherited it. She rented it at £140 per annum for fourteen years to two Liverpool theatre managers, Joseph Younger and George Mattocks. Sir William Chambers was selected to design the theatre, and he planned a stout, brick-fronted edifice, with a good-sized, simple entrance lobby. This led directly on to the boxes, which cost 3s 6d a performance, while passages on either side of the lobby led to the pit, at 2s 6d, and the gallery, at 1s a seat. The gallery was especially well-regarded at the time, and, in its early years, attracted a considerable upper-class clientèle. This was an unusual feature for a gallery, but it was noted how, quite spontaneously, the lower orders gravitated to the right, leaving the well-to-do to occupy the left-hand seating. In spite of its dignified façade, the theatre was somewhat squat and narrow in form, for extended depth was prevented by the rope works which occupied the present Chartres Street and St John's Market area. Soon after the opening of the theatre, the thirty shareholders granted a twenty-year lease to Mrs Bennett, so that in effect she enjoyed both building and performing rights.

On 5 June 1772 the theatre was ready, with that swiftness of construction which baffles the twentieth-century observer, used as he is to procrastination in these affairs. A long prologue was declaimed, penned in ripe, high-sounding Augustan couplets. One stanza ran:

> Long too has Mersey roll'd her golden tide,
> And seen proud vessels in her harbour ride;

Oft on her banks the Muse's sons would roam,
And wish'd to settle there a certain home;
Condemn'd, alas! to hawk unlicens'd bays,
Contraband mummeries, and unlicens'd plays!

The prologue also included a sincere tribute to the popular Gibson, whose spadework had led to the inception of legitimate theatre in the town. Then those first-nighters were regaled with a tidily balanced programme of the tragedy *Mahomet* and the farce *The Deuce is in Him*. A week later real-life tragedy struck the theatre when during the first of a strange series of false fire-alarms with which the theatre was to be inflicted, a man was killed and several injured. A woman died in similar circumstances in 1815.

The theatrical pattern was a neat one. In the summer the Drury Lane and Covent Garden theatres closed, and the players came north to the licensed theatres of Manchester and Liverpool. Alternately, the northern theatres normally closed in the winter months when the actors returned to London. It was not immediately a great financial success for the managers. Younger died in 1784 without making a great deal of profit, and Mattocks retired two years later a ruined man, leaving George Case to take up the lease and Francis Aickin to assume the shaky reins of management.

The history of the Theatre Royal turned out to be a counterpoint of exciting theatrical occasions and unpleasant, disconcerting happenings. The closing years of the eighteenth century were marked by instances of both. Elizabeth Farren began her career at the Theatre Royal in 1774, afterwards becoming a notable addition to the London stage. David Garrick wrote that 'she is much too fine stuff to be worn and soiled at Manchester and Liverpool', and, helping to initiate the grand tradition of actresses marrying into the aristocracy, she became the wife of the Earl of Derby. She died in 1829. In 1776 Garrick himself appeared in Jonson's *Every Man in his Humour*, while a year previously the theatre witnessed one of the first major provincial performances of the 'Messiah'. The year 1775 was also distinguished by the appearance of Charles Macklin as Macbeth, Richard III, and Shylock, while on 25 August *The Rivals* was given its first provincial showing. Macklin later introduced the famed W. C. Macready, who made his debut at the Theatre Royal in 1785 as the Duke of Suffolk in *Lady Jane Grey*. Mr and Mrs Siddons and her brother,

John Kemble, were welcome and frequent visitors to Liverpool in these years. In December 1877, for example, there was a star-studded version of *Hamlet*, with Sarah Siddons as a female Hamlet playing opposite Elizabeth Farren's Ophelia, with Kemble as Laertes, Siddons as Horatio and the theatre manager, Joseph Younger, as the Ghost. John Kemble was also for some time associated with the management of the theatre.

On the other side of the medallion there were discreditable, if no less fascinating, scenes. In 1778 an attempt to float a non-metropolitan, provincial company plummetted to disastrous failure. The absence of star names stimulated no local patriotism in the Liverpolitan theatre-goer. When the company opened in June, the auditorium walls were covered in verse and slogans attacking the new policy, and a riot prevented the performance. There were other troubles. In 1783 sailors introduced a bull taken from West Derby Wakes into the theatre, and another honest tar, some years later, leapt from gallery to stage determined to save the pretty Harriot Mellon from the villain of some hack melodrama. In 1797, when the local merchants had practised gunnery in anticipation of a French invasion, they were goaded by the galleryites, and so loudly prolonged were the taunts of 'charging guns with brown sugar and coconuts' and 'small arms with cinnamon powder and nutmegs' that Mrs Siddons had to perform in dumb show. Another, perhaps apocryphal, story of 1798 concerned the death of the actor, Palmer's son. The father was playing in *The Stranger*, and on speaking the prophetic line 'there is another and a better world', his sorrow overwhelmed him and he fell dead on the stage.

Over the latter years of the century the behaviour of the audiences was abominable. An especially unpleasant habit was that of urinating from the gallery into the boxes and pit. 'Several boxes', reported a local newspaper in 1795, 'were evacuated last night in consequence of the streams which descended from above, and some of the company in the pit had their clothes soiled in the same abominable manner.' A year or so later *The Monthly Mirror* claimed that 'the theatre is in a shameful condition', and their correspondent wrote: 'more turbulent, indecent and tasteless audiences, than have been met with here, have seldom, I believe, assembled within the precincts of any theatre, amphitheatre, barn, booth or stable', and in a later edition he claimed that 'the parsimony of the manager is still the subject of general complaint'.

The times were not propitious. The French wars were raging and this had some effect on the port, although it could hardly explain the shameful canvas against which some of the most notable doyens of the English stage were asked to perform. In thirty years the theatre had become a byword for riotous behaviour and tawdry production, and it was no surprise when the theatre closed on 24 November 1802. Boaden's *Voice of Nature*, *The Midnight Hour* and a burletta based on the tale of Tom Thumb formed the last programme, for which receipts were £241.

New brooms were soon sweeping clean. There was obviously a need for a good theatre in Liverpool, and, again with an amazing swiftness, the new theatre was ready for its reopening six months after the demise of the old. *The Monthly Mirror*, hitherto fiercely critical of the Theatre Royal, now felt able to eulogise on 'the most elegant, commodious, compact and chastely proportioned' theatre in England. It reflected great credit on the brave new managers, Messrs Lewis and Knight, and yet again hopes were high. The prologue, once more resplendent in velvety couplets, struck a soaring note of optimism:

> Our vessel is *royal*—the standard you view.
> Which can ne'er be pull'd down—while supported by you!

It was on 6 June that this encouraging prologue reopened the theatre, and the evening's programme was a happy one. *Speed the Plough* was a most popular play in Liverpool, and was enthusiastically received. This was followed by a jolly musical entitled *No Song, No Supper*. The grand semicircular auditorium constructed by the architect, Mr Foster, was much admired, and the New Theatre Royal thus started pleasantly.

Charles Mathews was the Regency equivalent of a matinée idol in Liverpool at this time, and his handsome features and brisk acting made him the chief theatrical attraction of the pre-Waterloo era. In 1814, however, John Vandenhoff made his début. Like Mathews, he was an actor who preferred to stake his career principally in the provinces, indeed in Liverpool. He was prepared to forego the temptations of London and its attendant risks for the security and muted glory of localised fame, and, although he is never mentioned in company with a Siddons or an Irving, for many years he sustained his huge following among the Liverpool theatre-goers. A well-built, blond and boldly good-looking man, he assuredly kept his place in the hearts of his fans for long enough.

Less popular, albeit very talented, was George Frederick Cooke. He earned himself a reputation as an alcoholic, and there is no denying his histrionic gifts were frequently impaired by his affection for the bottle. Stumbling through a drunken and slipshod performance of *Richard III* one evening, he was hissed noisily by the audience. It is said that he halted, looked at the audience, then prepared to leave. He paused at the exit and said very clearly, 'There is not a brick in your damned town but which is not cemented by the blood of a negro.' Naturally he never appeared again in Liverpool. This explicit reference, made as it were *in vino veritas*, to Liverpool's complicity in the slave trade struck home hard. It was, of course, a feature of Liverpool's commercial life never openly discussed, and merchants were always at great pains to point out that the slave ships never actually docked in Liverpool. Cooke's public repudiation of the taboo recalled an incident a quarter of a century earlier, when the play *Oroonoko* was banned because it reflected adversely on the slave trade and commented obliquely on Liverpool's participation in it. The theatre, then as now, offered some interesting political sidelights.

Apart from local heroes, nationally reputed actors and actresses came to the new Theatre Royal. Edmund Kean played a full Shakespearian season in the autumn of 1815, taking the lead in *Richard II*, *Richard III*, *The Merchant of Venice* (as Shylock), and *Othello*. It must have been an impressive virtuoso performance as the famous actor battled with such a disparate quartet. The following year John Kemble took his leave of his Liverpool fans with a farewell portrayal of *Coriolanus*. It was forty years since his début, and he had enjoyed a friendly response from Liverpool audiences during that lengthy spell. It is interesting to note that another Kemble—Fanny, presumably named after Mrs Siddons—first appeared in Liverpool in 1830 at the new Theatre Royal. That was in the same year that Ellen Tree and Charles Kean made their Liverpool débuts.

Two other internationally known artists performed at the theatre during these opening decades of the nineteenth century. One was the great clown, Joe Grimaldi. His first performance at the Theatre Royal was on 30 July 1817, as Bob Acres in Sheridan's *The Rivals*. It is perhaps a little surprising to hear of so famous a droll enjoying a huge success in a 'straight' role, but he was rapturously received. Over this period it was the custom to award benefit performances to an actor or actress, an occasion upon which they could claim an evening's profits for themselves. Grimaldi broke the record. He received a handsome bounty of £328, a very encouraging night's work given the value of money then. The theatre was, of course, occasionally used for musical and artistic ventures other than the purely dramatic, and much later, in the winter of 1832, Paganini enjoyed wide critical acclaim over a season of three concerts.

Once more a glittering parade of famous artists had its seamy side. The year 1810 in particular was one of disquiet, and much of the trouble centred on the Half-Price Riots. The management abandoned the cheaper prices to their detriment—there was much fighting, rowdyism, and vandalism as a result of their decision not to offer any seats at any time at half-price. Every single window in the theatre was broken, and six rioters were imprisoned. In these years Williamson Square had an unsavoury reputation, and the square and its surrounds were given over almost entirely to the commercial exploitation of vice, which could hardly have helped a theatre struggling for respectability. The nineteenth century was scarcely a theatrical heyday, and until the advent of Gilbert and Sullivan theatre-going was not quite as socially acceptable as it had been in Elizabethan London or Regency Bath. Despite its newness, the Theatre Royal was soon under heavy attack, notably in the *Liverpool Theatrical Investigator*. The press railed against the filthiness of the accommodation and the stinginess and appalling taste of the productions—a repetition of the former story.

The *Liverpool Theatrical Investigator* also trounced the Theatre Royal daily, its tiny four-page format maintaining a steady and virulent fire. 'The management are, it seems, determined', it told its readers in September 1821, 'to persevere in their wretched and despicable system.' This 'system' included ringing the changes daily over a relatively large number of plays, which the *Investigator* criticised each morning vehemently, and indeed, it is hard not to conclude that these plays must have been lamentably under-rehearsed. For example, the seven pieces performed over the nine days from Monday, 10 September to Tuesday, 18 September (the theatre was closed at the weekend) were *Virginius*, *Damon and Pythias* (twice), *Wallace*, *Rob Roy*, *Fazio* and *Macbeth*. It must have been difficult for the company to whirl at breakneck speed from Shakespeare and Greek tragedy to Highland melodrama.

The next step, and that not a happy one, was in the years 1842 and 1843. There was a long struggle with the Liver Theatre, whose manager was severely fined for his insistence on offering legitimate presentations which infringed the patent of the Theatre Royal. The row eventually led to legislation. As with so many other institutions, the Victorians found time for theatrical reform; in 1843 an Act for the Regulation of Theatres was passed. It ended the patents that had protected the Theatres Royal for so long, and the new Theatre Royal lost its traditional privileges. Now it had to compete on equal terms with the theatres that began to sprout in the town.

But the Theatre Royal stumbled on for another forty years. An odd happening in 1847 was the appearance of Charles Dickens in a benefit performance of *Every Man in His Humour*. Dickens, an eager and gifted amateur actor, sometimes indulged himself at the professional level, and on 28 July, like Garrick before him, he performed in Jonson's satirical comedy, in the very summer when the Irish migrations reached their height and disease was rampant through the streets.

It is strange to imagine Dickens on the stage of the Theatre Royal in the year that the social terrors of Liverpool low life had dropped to what was possibly their nadir. Twenty years later Charles Dickens was to reappear at the Theatre Royal when, in the April of 1869, he gave one of his world-famous readings to a full and delighted audience.

Several other exciting events brightened the dimness of the theatre's decline. In 1860 Henry Irving, probably the best known of Victorian actors, made his Liverpool début in *Faust and Marguerite*. The year 1856 saw two quite dissimilar firsts. In September, rather early in the year by modern standards, the new Theatre Royal's first pantomime was staged. This was *Jack and the Beanstalk*, starring Madame Celeste, a noted soubrette of the day, as principal boy. On 21 October the first production in Liverpool of *La Traviata* was presented. Then, in the summer of 1866, there appeared the American Slave Serenaders, part of the opening phases of the long tradition of 'nigger minstrels', in the style of the Christie Minstrels, the Kentucky Minstrels, Al Jolson and, latterly, the Black and White Minstrels. They were billed as 'the only combination of genuine darkies in the world'. One wonders whether anyone reflected on the irony of a slave troupe entertaining in the town which had itself contributed to that infamous trade. Again, the context was gloomy, for in that summer the last of the great cholera epidemics raged in Liverpool.

Despite its occasional splendours, the Theatre Royal had always been an unstable and struggling institution. By 1884 it could barely support any kind of theatrical venture, and it was adapted as a circus, but within a year this too had failed, and the Theatre Royal went out of commission. The mention of Henry Irving, of minstrel shows and pantomimes, is a reminder that the theatre in general was on the threshold of a highly colourful and successful period, especially in the field of light entertainment. For a little over a hundred years the Theatre Royal had managed to sustain itself, and it was sad that its final collapse, not unexpected, should come as live theatre began a hearty era of success. It had been a hundred years of tribulation, and there had been a theatrical flavour about its own history. Behind the glitter of the Kembles and the Siddonses, of Irving, Macklin, and Matthews, of Ellen Tree and Elizabeth Farren, there was a hard reality of maladministration, inconsistent support, and unpleasant conditions. Like the plays themselves, the Theatre Royal was a façade behind which managers struggled endlessly to make ends meet, until the curtain fell ineluctably both on actors and management.

It had not, of course, been a happy century for the theatre. Ireland may have sent many thousands to Liverpool in the nineteenth century, but in the whole era between Sheridan and Wilde or Shaw, she sent no other dramatist, and the English could scarcely muster one of their own. Contemporary drama was at its most turgid level. Prudishness and vulgarity existed side by side with vile, punning comedy and clumsy, ill-rehearsed performance. The minstrel troupes aside, the only worthwhile musical entertainments were foreign opera, and the provinces saw little or nothing of these at any reasonable level of presentation.

In illustration of this factor, one might quote from the Amphitheatre pantomime of 1861. It was *The Old Woman who lived in a Shoe* or *The Harlequin Child of Childwall* and *The Christmas Spirits of Dingley Dell*. The affection for lengthy titles was further demonstrated by the synopsis of scenes: 'Scene V. Everton Village; Molly Bushell's Toffy Shop, Ancient Cross etc. (from Herdman's *Ancient Liverpool*) the remains of this cross are preserved in the round house on Everton Brow'. The scene began:

Enter the Old Woman and her children.

DAME: They've turned me out of my old shoe, to roam,
And play at 'hunt the slipper' for a home.
So far my search is *bootless*—Hard it is!
For rents run high and water rates is riz.
O, if I catch that farmer, I declares,
I'll knock his head off.

BOY: Aye, and Suriganswares!

DAME: Their hearts are hard, if they have hearts at all,
As those four lions at St George's Hall.

BOY: Keep up your pecker, Mother, never fret;

2ND BOY: Here's Farmer Nightshade,

1ST BOY: We'll cook *his goose* yet.

So it continued for a long, full performance, rather in the manner of perhaps a Sunday-school children's Christmas entertainment today. One could possibly enjoy the agony of a ten- or fifteen-minute sketch in this style, but for a whole evening's entertainment in a major provincial theatre it was tedious and wearing. This is not the assessment of one forgetful of changed fashions of humour; this kind of theatre was not deeply approved of nor widely supported in its own epoch.

Apart from trivial farce, empty burlesque and hollow melodrama, Shakespeare provided the staple diet. Season after season the chief Shakespearian plays were rehashed and built around some visiting thespian potentate. In a manner florid and hyperbolic for modern taste, the famed actors of the day would strut and preen their way through *Hamlet* or *Macbeth*.

As the century wore on, matters changed a little, apart from the welcome recrudescence of strong contemporary writing by such as Ibsen or Shaw. Gilbert and Sullivan initiated a minor theatrical revolution. Their admirable composition of wit and melody, pleasingly compounded in an unerringly tasteful and sensible style, wrought a significant change in theatrical climate. They made theatre-going at once respectable and enjoyable, not so simple a challenge as it appears. It is also sometimes forgotten that Gilbert's habit of systematic and disciplined production had

an important effect in the theatre. The slipshod and messy direction of the past decades, with its over-reliance on flashy spectacle,
was replaced by Gilbertian method. The theatre became a place
of middle-class entertainment, and Gilbert and Sullivan might
claim that their work enlisted a seminal support which extended
down the years to provide audiences for a whole lineage of musical
plays and revues from Romberg and Léhar to Rogers and Ham-
merstein. Gilbert and d'Oyly Carte inaugurated the competent
school of producers, ironing out shoddiness and buffooneries, concentrating on accurate, well-bred presentation not only in acting but
in scenic and costume design. Moreover, they also insisted, unlike
the owners of the Theatre Royal, on clean and gracious accommodation. Gradually the theatre became an agreeable resort
for the ordinary man and his family, a place of comfort and
pleasure.

Another tradition was at the same time becoming respectable.
The music-hall or variety theatre had started life in the taverns
and singing-rooms, and naturally it was frowned upon by the
prim Victorian businessman and the respected tradesman. Its rich
vigour proved healthy enough for music-hall to blossom forth,
so that, in its prime, a city like Liverpool had several variety
theatres in action. The two strands—the respectable musical and
the respectable music-hall—somehow joined to inaugurate a
golden age of English light entertainment, an epoch not to be
ended until cinema, and then radio, and lastly television in turn
reached their maturity, a maturity itself heavily reliant on the
substance of the live theatre.

As the Theatre Royal died, other theatres were established to
envelop the new, bright ripeness of music-hall and a revitalised
legitimate theatre. The Amphitheatre had been built in 1825, but
it was not until it was reopened and re-christened as the Royal
Court in 1881 that it flourished properly. Like so many north-
western houses, it was owned by the highly successful Manchester
impresario, Bainbridge, and the Bainbridge circuit was an envied
spot for performers at the turn of the century and after.

The new theatres brought to Liverpool the famous performers
of the age, many of them still household words. The Adelphi was
opened in 1846 and in 1867 Dan Leno made his first appearance
in Liverpool there. The Shakespeare Theatre, now adapted as a
theatre club, was opened in 1888 and at Christmas, 1900, possibly

Page 35   The Theatre Royal, until recently a cold-storage depot, and the nearby Playhouse Theatre, with its brand-new restaurant

Page 36 The famous Empire Theatre, one of Liverpool's only two remaining commercial theatres

the most famous of variety stars, George Robey, played in *Jack and the Beanstalk* there. But the most notable of Merseyside's variety theatres was not in Liverpool at all. It was the Argyll, Birkenhead, perhaps the most well-known provincial music-hall in its day; it was under the able management of Dennis Clarke and only recently has it ceased its lengthy connection with live entertainment.

Apart from the Royal Court there is only one other commercial house in Liverpool, although two repertory companies are still extant. The other survivor is the Empire on Lime Street. It began life in 1866 as the Royal Alexandra, and then as now its main bread-winner was a long-running pantomime. Where last year Charlie Drake starred in panto, Vesta Tilley was principal boy in *Sinbad the Sailor* in 1886. It was in 1896 that the theatre was renamed with its present title. In that year it was taken over by Moss Empires, another successful circuit that has lasted to the present period. Predictably, it began life as the Empire with a pantomime, *Cinderella*, and it was a few years later at the Empire that Harry Tate discovered Tommy Tweedley, who became the addle-pated son in Tate's motoring sketch, surely the most priceless of all music-hall cameos.

In 1912 variety reached its apotheosis with the first-ever Royal Command Performance. At this time Liverpool had several music-halls, and the selected stars were well known to Merseyside audiences: Vesta Tilley, Harry Tate, Little Tich as 'the Game-keeper', Clarice Mayne, Anna Pavlova, Wilkie Bard ('I want to sing in Opera'), Harry Lauder, Arthur Prince, and George Robey as 'the Mayor of Mudcumdyke'.

It is fascinating to glance at a variety programme for that same year at the Liverpool Empire. After the overture, 'The Merry Wives of Windsor', the bill was opened with George Newburn, 'the popular imitator of popular stars'. The impressionist has been a stable, if minor, species of the variety stage, and radio was to give a useful boost to this type of act. After some years of decline, it seems to have been rejuvenated recently on television. George Rapley, a comedian, followed, and the third act was the Eisteddfod Sextette Prize Vocalists, hardly the catchy or off-beat title to which modern ears have grown used. As the intermission, an American Bioscope offered 'a new series of uptodate subjects'. It was the beginning of cinema, and it is interesting to note that, when the cinema began in earnest, it was to lace its offerings with live acts, just as the Empire had the bioscope as an added attraction. After the interval Belle Davis and her Crackerjacks danced their way through 'Southern Pastimes', and then a comic well known in his day, Bert Coote, starred in *The Eternal Waltz*, 'a music (h)al(l) comedy'. The musical burlesque, sometimes called a 'song-chainer', was another feature of the halls, and once more it was a type of humour repeated to the present day, occasionally in a sophisticated revue form. The same is true of the comedy duo. The double act was just coming into its own, and it was to reach its heyday in the thirties and forties. It had a successful transatlantic offshoot, in films as well as in vaudeville, and in the talented hands of such as Morecambe and Wise*, the tradition is safe today. Camp and Critic were the Empire's double act on this occasion, and they presented 'a screaming farce' entitled 'Waxworks'. The last two acts have not worn so well. There was Probst, Whistler and Mimic. The whistler, like the yodeller, seems today to be in the shadows. Finally, there was Fred Maitland and Company in 'a farcical extravaganza' excruciatingly called 'Roots, Rash Chemist'. The comedian and a supporting troupe is not so prevalent a type of act nowadays, but the popular Fred Maitland was working the same kind of turn as notables like Harry Tate and Fred Karno.

A theatre programme was always a rich source of incidental information. 'Cycles stored free of charge' was an offer that placed the time neatly in the transitional period before motoring had taken a firm hold and after the carriage had begun to decline in import. Jeyes Fluid was vigorously advertised in the programme, while Budden & Co recommended their throat medicine 'Pynod', at 10½d a bottle, 'the breathable remedy'.

The Empire was not the only theatre, of course. By the turn of the century there were as well as the Empire, the Royal Court, the Star, the Shakespeare, the Rotunda, the Lyric, the Queens, the Grand, and others. *Smith's Liverpool Weekly* faithfully reported on all their doings. In 1904, for instance, Hetty King was Dick Whittington at the Royal Court and Carrie Moore was Aladdin at the Shakespeare; Eugene Stratton and the celebrated Marie Lloyd both appeared at the Empire during the year, while Henry

* Morecambe and Wise made their début as a double act at the Empire.

The Theatre Royal and after

Irving played the Shakespeare. 'In the Liverpool halls', said the 1904 *Annual of Smith's Liverpool Weekly* a trifle sententiously, 'we get the genus music hall entertainment at its best—free from offence, harmless, blithe and restorative.'

It was too late, however, to restore the Theatre Royal. The unlucky Theatre Royal missed the limelight, and it is strange that this most notable of Liverpool's theatres thus managed to eke out its existence throughout a veritable theatrical doldrums. As with any commentary on Liverpolitan theatrical history, these observations lean heavily on the painstaking work of the admirable R. J. Broadbent, once the unremitting chronicler of the Merseyside stage, and, in particular, on his *Annals of the Liverpool Stage*, published in 1908. The Victorian antiquarians were doubtless a little lacking in perception and flair, but a huge debt is owed them for their indefatigable collation. From this it is possible to extract the items of interest as well as some continuous theme. Later, the Theatre Royal, whose activities Broadbent catalogued so affectionately, was a cold-storage depot, fittingly enough, for coldness has inspired many a stage metaphor for failure. Realism had triumphed at last. And, just a few days ago, the whole building, pictured on page 35, was razed to the ground.

CHAPTER TWO

The first Grand National

Sport is more patchy on Merseyside than the inhabitants care to admit. Two successful football teams overshadow all, although both, whisper it gently, have suffered the doldrums of the second division since the war. Rugby Union enjoys a brisk first-class support, but it is not a rugby region to place alongside South Wales, the Midlands, south-west England, the Scots border or the home counties. Rugby League has never really won a foothold, despite the success of nearby Wigan, St Helens, Leigh, and Warrington. Cricket, so strong in Lancashire, centres on Manchester and tends to find a healthier backing in the eastern reaches of the county. Liverpool has its fine roll of honour of boxing, like many another port, but certain other sports—tennis, athletics, swimming, greyhound racing, rowing, to mention only a few, do not traditionally find a significant locus on Merseyside. The long foreshores of the Dee and Mersey estuaries make golf something of an exception, and, out of a dozen clubs, Royal Birkdale and Royal Liverpool at Hoylake are pre-eminent, while the West Lancashire club at Crosby is reputed to be the oldest in the county. This and football apart, there remains but the Grand National to save Liverpool's reputation as a sporting hub of the nation. Indeed, it is Liverpool's sole regular contribution to the sporting calendar of the country, but so famous is it that it is additionally one of the nation's major contributions to world sport; the Grand National is the world's premier steeplechase.

There have been alarms and fears, not least these last few years when, like some ageing actress, the Grand National has enjoyed positively its last performance several times. For over a hundred years the crowds have flocked out to Aintree to witness the spectacle, usually only fleetingly, unless the comfort and vantage point of the grandstand can be afforded. For the run-of-the-mill spectator, camped out in the 'wide open world' it is two exciting, noisy, blurred blotches of colour and horseflesh and then a long wait for rumour to permeate round the course, or, in these times, the more instant accuracy of the transistor radio. Television offers the armchair racegoer a more faithful and complete record, but as with most great race-days, rubber-necking and sniffing the atmosphere is an important element. The usual raggle-taggle of tipsters, fortune-tellers and pedlars is in abundance, with the complement of mobile catering vans and busy bars. The book-makers are the pleasantest surprise. They so closely resemble the caricatured bookies of the third-rate stage or the boy's comic, with Gladstone bags bulging over with notes, florid faces, cigars, blackboards, half-empty pint glasses and with the incessantly sig-nalling tic-tac men dancing frenzied attendance. And it is true that one sees the famous there, although today's spectator is more likely to spot and eagerly point out the famed of film and television than of the House of Lords. Royalty has intermittently supported the National. A popular story in the Ormskirk and Aintree area is that the royal train used to park overnight at nearby Aughton, where banks of turf (so the legend ran) with flowerpots cleverly buried were carefully constructed on either side of the appropriate carriage, so that the royals, when rising and breakfasting, could enjoy the illusion of their train having meandered into an English country garden.

Racing can certainly be a great leveller. Over the years it has often managed to be both exclusive and classless, both intolerably snobbish and broadminded. Probably its snobbishness has oper-ated as a unifier, just as Jeeves' pride in the Woosters is of steelier mettle than Bertie's. The horse has enjoyed a very long history of athletic involvement, its military use along with its value in the hunt ensuring that man, at leisure, has turned to apposite eques-trian pursuits. The hunt fulfilled a number of functions. It pro-vided food or the riddance of vermin, it provided social focus and enjoyment, it provided would-be cavalrymen with experience in competitive horsemanship and in observation of terrain. In the early decades of the last century the horse was as much a common denominator as the mass had been in medieval times, linking all classes in a common reverence and interest. Everyone who could rode and everyone else aspired to ride or at least to be included in the vast army of camp-followers. Ostlers, grooms, and stable-lads were everywhere; each hunt recruited its staunch regiment of whippers-in and dog-stoppers. 'Regency England', wrote Arthur Bryant, 'stank of the stable and was proud of it.'

The onset of industrialism was not as yet halting this proclivity, and it even stimulated some aspects of horse utility. Factories and docks and mines used horses and ponies, and a factory-lad would need to be capable of tending his employer's mounts. The canals, such as the Leeds and Liverpool canal, were at the peak of their prominence and this in turn meant a regular trade in chain-horses and the manufacture and maintenance of their equipment. It was also the epoch of England's great coach-builders, for the gentry maintained an amazing variety of carriages, with makes almost as multifarious as those of the car in our century. It was the day of the flying mail-coaches, thundering in resplendent array over the new highways of the kingdom. When railways took over, the horse was not neglected, for horses were required at terminal points and also initially for assistance at gradients, travelling in recuperative ease in dandy-boxes whilst the engine chugged over the flat. It was a two-way world. If the huntsman found common ground with his master, the young bloods aped the mannerisms of the professional coachmen. Horsemanship and coachmanship were outstanding social cachets in what was truly the day of 'the fraternity of the curry-comb'.

It was also the age of the bully-boy English, delighting in manly, frequently brutal pastimes, delighting as often in uproarious, boisterous, frivolous sport and delighting in gamey, plucky blood and breeding. 'A sort of grown children', was how William Hazlitt described them. Strangely, the Englishman was supposed to be honest about all matters excepting the horse, where shady dealing was surprisingly accepted; it helped, it was argued, the young man to learn to stand on his own feet and develop what was called 'horse-sense'. Thus a gallon of ale to quieten a vicious mount or a live eel to enliven a pacific one were customs taken for granted, while in the Liverpool and Preston areas 'feiging' was not uncommon—the practice, that is, of inserting a piece of ginger into a horse's rump to produce a show of exhilaration.

All these elements fused in horse-racing. There was the love of an ubiquitous presence of the horse, there was the itch for sporty pleasures accompanied by wagers and bets to the extent that Weatherby's and Tattersalls were soon national institutions, there was horse-trading, and the legitimate use, still customary, of the horse-race to demonstrate a horse's worth. It was a rumbustious and ill-regulated sport, with a broad-ranging scope for devious manoeuvres of sundry kinds. The turf had already established its classic races. Sir Charles Bunbury's 'Diomed' had won the first Derby as early as 1780, and, before the first Grand National, Lord Egremont, like the Aga Khan in this century, had owned five Derby winners. Even earlier the Doncaster St Leger was first run in 1776 and the Oaks three years afterwards. The other two classics—the One Thousand and Two Thousand Guineas—were first run over the Rowley Mile at Newmarket in 1814 and 1809 respectively.

Flat-racing was more legitimate than steeplechasing by a short head. It had been organised for a longer period, with Charles II —old Rowley himself—reputed to have handled the ribbons at Newmarket. Steeplechasing had existed from the early decades of the eighteenth century, and it had literally been a chase, usually of two horses for a private wager, to and from given church steeples. As a spectator sport it properly came into prominence at St Alban's under the jurisdiction of Tom Coleman, who as well as being possibly the first to introduce the steeplechase to the public was also the first to be ruined by so precarious an enterprise. For his precedent, seized upon and developed at Aintree, was to see the eclipse of the once popular St Alban's steeplechasing.

There was some slight tradition in the north-west. A four-mile race has been recorded at Crosby in 1776, and, in the post-Waterloo era, Blackburn was the location of a March steeplechase meeting, probably organised with Tom Coleman's aid. On the whole, however, the Merseyside bucks had to migrate to Epsom, Doncaster, St Alban's and Newmarket for the finest sport, yet within years Liverpool was destined to house one of those few sporting encounters which, like the Eton and Harrow Match at Lord's, became essential dates in the aristocratic social whirl.

Suddenly, out of little or nothing, there were two competing race-courses so close physically that commentators have not surprisingly failed to distinguish clearly between them, and have believed the one substantially to have overlapped the other. In 1827 John Formby began race-meetings at Maghull, no more than a mile or so from Aintree. His father-in-law had bought the land from the old-established and wealthy Molyneux family, and with the backing of a notable committee with Molyneux representation, racing commenced. In July 1829 William Lynn, landlord of the Waterloo Hotel at Aintree, also established a racetrack not far, for obvious reasons, from his hostelry. He had leased land from the same Molyneux family, and his patron was Lord Molyneux, heir to the Sefton earldom, one of the leading Lancastrian noble escutcheons. The difference between these two enterprising gentlemen and the ordinary run of racing organisers lay in their consideration and deliberate courtship of the public, for instead of the usual headlong helter-skelter, with only the runners aware of the destination and prize, both were determined to mount a spectacle. To this end they were intent on establishing some kind of comprehensible circuit, with the runners beginning and finishing in roughly the same spot, for the convenience of viewers. Lynn built a grandstand for this purpose before any racing was held at Aintree, and Formby promised one at Maghull, although it is not certain whether this was completed or not.

Like Formby, Lynn was primarily interested in flat-racing, and it was seven years before he turned his attention to steeplechasing. By this time—in 1835, more or less—Maghull had conceded his victory to Aintree, and John Formby was a disappointed and bitter man. Some turf histories describe the first three Grand Nationals as having been run at Maghull; one at least implies that the two courses were conjoined for the purpose. Neither of these presuppositions are true; Maghull was no longer a going concern when the first Grand National was battled out, and as deadly rivals, one a tenant and one a leaseholder with distinct slots of land, it is most unlikely that the early Nationals touched Maghull at all. What seals this conclusion is a little-known document, called *An Account of the Liverpool Races*, printed by Formby himself and published as early as 1828. To his amazement and dismay no sooner had he commenced races at Maghull than the Aintree enterprise was mooted. This happened within weeks. Moreover, it was the committee established to organise the Maghull races who were supporting the plan, and seemingly their first decision was to contemplate a move to Aintree, almost before Maghull had been used at all. The committee included many of the local nobility, including the Earl of Sefton, and Formby could barely believe the gentry could prove to be the vipers within his bosom. In his pamphlet he ostentatiously refused to believe the reports, as he felt no English nobleman could stoop to such treacherous behaviour. The committee, he argued, had been appointed for the especial purpose of managing Maghull race-meetings, and to contemplate a transfer was 'an assumption of illegitimate authority'. He promised a grandstand and other amenities and swore that 'nothing shall put a stop to the Liverpool races at Maghull'. It was an idle oath. His errant committee and William Lynn outflanked him from the onset, and struggle though he did for six seasons, Formby never managed to put Maghull races on the mat. Why the committee at first sight of John Formby or his races turned immediately and abruptly on him cannot firmly be decided. Possibly his abrasive personality, evidenced in this published pamphlet, or a practical inefficiency not recorded for posterity, was the cause. Again, it may have been Lynn's superior salesmanship.

The remaining question is: which actually was the first Grand National? According to interpretation, it could have been in 1836, 1839, just possibly 1843, or 1847. William Lynn certainly organised a steeplechase for the first time in 1836. This was a four-mile route with twenty fences and two hurdles both in the straight, intended for 'gentlemen' and with twelve stones as the standard weight demanded. The race began and ended at the new grandstand, the competitors covering the circuit twice. It was severe running over ploughland and the boundaries were indicated by field borders and hedges. The fences too were natural, being simply the normal agricultural hazards of hedge and ditch with the exception of the two hurdles. It was planned at the end of the hunting season as a selling race, a trial run for hunters from which the winner was to be sold for £300, a fair price at a time when a pound a week was regarded as an average wage. There were ten runners. It was a slow time, as riders tended to explore fences searching for strategic points to jump, this being the convention for some time and obviously one of the chief differences between the present day and then. In a not-too-well-documented race the famous Captain Becher won on 'The Duke'.

It was a successful function and the following year the Liverpool corporation gave Lynn a hundred pounds' subsidy. The race was advertised as a £10 sweepstake, with £180 added. The weighting became a little more sophisticated; four-year-olds carried eleven stones, five-year-olds eleven and a half stones, and six-year-olds and over, twelve stones. Foolishly, the race was programmed the day after the St Alban's meeting and the field was wretchedly reduced to a mere four, Captain Becher being a notable absentee. The setting at Liverpool was ideal, which made the poor field the more disappointing, as there was a goodish crowd, comprehensive press coverage, and Lynn's patron, Viscount Molyneux, acting as umpire. It was in this year that Lynn's influence began to make itself felt in the racing world; he insisted on punctuality and orderliness, he was particularly careful about the precision of the start. In a sport haunted by and riddled with sharp practice, the accepted vacillations of times, distances and the like offered a welcome scope to enterprising cheats, not only in terms of winning prize-money, but with regard to bets, side-wagers and so forth.

There was in fact a false start and the runners were sternly recalled. A broken stirrup next held up the proceedings, but eventually the horses 'got off', it is reported, 'pretty fairly'. 'Dan O'Connell' was the favourite and he made the early running from his three rivals, 'The Duke', 'The Disowned', and 'Zanga'. Part way through the course was the Trial Fence, which as its name suggests subjected horse and jockey to their severest test. It was a wide ditch alongside six feet of thorn, and every horse had the good sense to refuse this frightening obstacle. 'Dan O'Connell' disappointed his many backers by sustaining his reticence to attempt the Trial Fence, but at a second attempt, 'The Duke' overcame it. Two hundred yards behind, 'The Disowned' eventually followed suit. 'Zanga', quite some minutes later, also jumped the Trial Fence, but unluckily fell at the next barrier and was withdrawn. Alan McDonough drove 'The Disowned' desperately after 'The Duke', who had seemed to have easily made the race his. 'The pace now became very severe'—according to the *Liverpool Standard*—'. . . the horses were nearly abreast, the riders punishing them severely.' The effort of overtaking the leader sapped 'The Disowned's' strength, and at the last 'The Duke' won 'by about thirty lengths at a severe pace'. The time was a much improved fifteen minutes—swift going over Aintree's ploughed acres. 'The Duke', a hunting cob owned by William Sirdefield of the George Inn was ridden by a popular Denbighshire jockey, Henry Potts, a twenty-seven-year-old competitor who had only accepted the ride latterly on the withdrawal through ill health of the chosen rider.

The first Grand National

The hard, cruel character of the Aintree steeplechase raised considerable opposition. Those not present read of the harsh punishment meted out to the horses by their over-eager riders. The humanitarian and evangelical mood of the nineteenth century was just taking shape, to which both an essential kindliness of spirit and a puritanical zealotry contributed, and it was manifest in a variety of social fields such as anti-child-labour campaigns and temperance movements. Given the Englishman's affection for the animal kingdom, it is not unexpected to discover a society for the 'Preventing of Wanton Cruelty to Brute Animals' in existence as early as 1808 in the Liverpool area. In 1823 'Humanity' Martin, with indispensable support from Lord Erskine, negotiated his Ill-treatment of Horses Act through Parliament. This produced a crop of fines and imprisonments, but it was widely believed that a dual standard existed. Coachmen and carters, trying to meet the unreasonable demands of their masters and clients, were suffering from this legislation, while the gentry, frantically whipping their horses through mad hunting adventures, went scot-free. In 1824 the Society for the Prevention of Cruelty to Animals was formed, and in 1840, by no coincidence, in the early years of Victoria's reign, it obtained royal patronage.

It may be recalled that some years ago a public outcry resulted in the easing of the monstrous challenge of the Grand National. Many steeplechasers, including perhaps the most famous of them all, 'Arkle', have never been risked over Aintree's tiring course. It has always been noted as a race that asked the utmost, possibly that and more, of jumper and jockey, and as a result it was from the beginning subjected to close scrutiny and loud criticism. Animal defenders, stung by accusations of dual standards, seized on what seemed to them a deliberately premeditated public exhibition of cruelty to attack the gentry for their harshness to their mounts. Because of this uproarious criticism, the town council withdrew its support hurriedly. Only £25 was added in 1838 to the £10 sweepstake, and Lynn, bowing to the SPCA and other assaults, lowered and eased several of the fences. Captain Becher rode 'The Duke' this year and it was two to one favourite. This time, however, Alan McDonough went one better than in 1837. His chestnut gelding 'Sir William' (not 'Sir Henry' as some record books maintain) was the victor, with 'Scamp' second, and the game 'The Duke' third. It was the first Irish win, the first owner-rider win, and 'The Duke', broken by his gallant labours, was the race's first major casualty, which of course did not escape the notice of Aintree's vociferous critics.

Just prior to the 1839 meeting, Lynn abruptly announced his retirement, ostensibly on the grounds of ill health but, in private correspondence, he bemoaned what he termed 'a most unlucky speculation'. Like Tom Coleman and his own rival John Formby, William Lynn found it difficult to make steeplechasing profitable. It was popular enough, but the public's outlay was not necessarily directed toward the promoter. Few paid to watch the race, and the business of transporting, catering, betting and entertaining did not automatically fall into Lynn's province. Equally one might ponder on the uneconomic maintenance of a grandstand, a race-course and all its impedimenta for what amounted to a quarter of an hour a year. In his statement to the public Lynn announced that the management of the race would pass to a group of in-fluential aristocrats and gentlemen of the turf well positioned to ensure 'the future arrangements of the races on a more secure and permanent footing'. The syndicate read like a page torn from *Debrett*; Lord Stanley, the Earls of Derby, of Eglington, of Wilton and of Sefton, and Lord George Bentinck were chief among them. It was a wealthy syndicate of a thousand shareholdings or 'proprieterships', each valued at twenty-five sovereigns. Lord George Bentinck was, in racing terms, the most influential of this titled company. With Admiral Rous he was instrumental in estab-lishing the Jockey Club, which was to do so much for the regula-tion of horse-racing in this country, and like Lynn, he was a firm believer in precise, orderly organisation for the convenience of the racegoers and the thwarting of the foxy fringe. Punctuality, num-bering, a proper starting system, a stern check both on weighing-in and weighing-out found in him, as in Lynn, enthusiastic encour-agement as they gradually became part of the Aintree scene and helped to propagate the gospel of disciplined racing. In 1844 Bentinck personally unmasked the notorious 'running rein' fraud perpetrated by several dishonest jockeys.

For their first venture they made the race a £20 sweepstake and added £100. A £5 forfeiture clause was added, and, as only seventeen of the fifty-three entries came under starter's orders, another £180 income was earned. The selling provision was dropped for the first time. The rules were tightened—one highly descriptive ruling commanded that no rider should 'open a gate or ride through a gateway or more than a hundred yards along any road, footpath or driftway'. In 1839 the 'gentlemen' tag enunciated by Lynn was abandoned; in any case it had most probably been abused. Eight professional jockeys—one-half the complement—rode in the 1839 race. These innovations, coupled with the controversy over venue, have led some commentators and turf archivists to call it the first Grand National, their case helped by the term 'Grand National' being unofficially coined for the first time in 1839 by an anonymous pressman.

There was also a breakthrough in public attention. The earlier years had been successful enough, but the 1839 meeting drew an estimated crowd of 50,000, a quite incredible number for that era. St Alban's was indeed finished, and Liverpool was already England's main steeplechasing centre. High society recognised this, doubtless encouraged by the blue-blooded character of the management committee. For a week beforehand the stately homes of Liverpool and South Lancashire were alight with feastings and junketings on an unprecedented and elaborate scale, and for the first time, not just many, but practically all the socialites poured into Merseyside for a week of banquets, dances, and parties, all prefacing the momentous events of the steeplechase. Stand seats were seven shillings, extravagantly expensive for the money values of the thirties. 'Piemen, chimney sweeps, cigar sellers, thimble-riggers and all the small fry of gaming-table keepers' joined the swarm of humanity descending, via a crazy assortment of conveyances, on Aintree. As the *Liverpool Courier* quaintly put it, 'our inns have been crowded with gentle and simple'.

They were not disappointed. They became restless during an unaccountable two-hour delay, a lengthy delay such as was very common and much disliked by William Lynn, and which was usually caused by latecomers, by argument over rulings and by tactical manoeuvres at the start. During this very long delay Alan McDonough put in 'some severe galloping' on 'The Nun', apparently in an attempt to condition her wind for the race. In spite of this tough treatment, 'The Nun' started as six to one favourite, good odds indicative of the openness of the race.

The initial phases of the race made history. Captain Becher led on 'Conrad' and they set off 'at a spanking pace'. At a paling surmounted by 'a high jagged hedge' and behind that a six-foot ditch, Becher was thrown. Old Becher, 'the last of the leather breeches', had a Wellingtonian reputation for falling and remounting, but on this occasion his fall etched for him a posterity denied to most of the victors. That murky trickle became Becher's Brook and the label stuck. 'Conrad' and Becher fell and 'rolled over into the brook', yet the determined captain thought not a jot for posterity; he dragged his horse struggling to its feet, pulled himself into the saddle and careered off after the new leaders. Remarkably, he reached and overtook them, but poor 'Conrad' decided he 'had no mind for such exertion' and at the next water-jump he fell irrevocably.

'Lottery' took up the challenge from 'The Nun' and 'Paulina'. 'Dictator' came suddenly into contention, took the lead, and then as abruptly tumbled. Despite an obvious strain, the unfortunate horse was remounted and driven at the next leap. It broke its back and died in a sorry attempt to clear the jump, and 'Dictator' became the National's first fatality. 'Lottery' went on to win handsomely from 'Seventy-four' with 'Paulina' third. 'The Nun' fell away in the closing stages, and, as McDonough ruefully said, 'Lottery' could 'trot faster than any of the rest of us could gallop'.

'Lottery' had been bought as a bargain at a provincial horse-fair and he became one of the most popular horses of all time, having that peculiar cast of equine personality that proves compulsive to the racing public. Heavily burdened with extra weight in future races, he never won the National again, but crowds turned out religiously to cheer him on. No sentimental pasture awaited him, for 'the greatest horse in the world' ended his long life between a carter's shaft. Jem Mason, 'the horsey dandy', invariably rode him and together they had won the Grand National. Mason took the precaution of marrying the daughter of John Elmore, 'Lottery's' owner. 'Lottery' apparently detested the dapper Mason, and he had to mount the horse from the rear—it is said that 'Lottery' kicked down a stable door in temper when, aged twenty, he heard Jem Mason's voice outside.

Whether or not it was the first Grand National, the 1839 steeplechase settled the future of Aintree, and its success was brilliantly assured. In 1840 the race was proudly heralded as the Grand Liverpool Steeplechase, but this proved to be a disastrous event, strewn with accidents. Only five of the thirteen starters finished, with 'Jerry', ridden by B. Bretherton, the winner. A reduced field and the absence of some of the aristocracy was explained by the Queen's marriage, motivating a whole series of social engagements that rather left the remainder of the season's events in the shadows. This was also the year that Valentine's Brook was named after an unfortunate horse that fell there. So many accidents obviously supplied the critics with substantial ammunition. *The Liverpool Mercury* was the main protagonist. It was a liberalised Whig newspaper, much given to supporting the rational reforms of the Grey and later Whig ministries, applauding, for instance, the Poor Law Amendment Act or the Registration of Births, Deaths and Marriages. Probably the High Tory connections of Aintree's patrons—Bentinck, Derby and the like —added to the *Mercury*'s scorn, and while its editorial staff regarded the National as cruel and foolish, the Tory *Liverpool Courier* was as predictably exhilarated by the occasion.

In 1841 A. Powell won on 'Charity', and then, in the two succeeding years, Black Tom Oliver was victorious on 'Gay Lad' in 1842 and 'Vanguard' in 1843. Black Tom was a popular fancy, admired alike by lord and commoner, perhaps the first in the small exclusive band of jockey-heroes, along with Archer, Donoghue, Richards, Piggott and only a handful more. Oliver was a dashing hard-living man as well as a gifted horseman. The public, as might be expected, loved this cavalier mélange of daredevil champion and *bon viveur*—when on one occasion incarcerated in Oxford prison for debt he told a friend he needed 'a good wall jumper'.

The 1843 race, known as the Liverpool and National Steeplechase, was chiefly significant for its being a handicap race, thus assuming its present form. William Lynn was still involved in the Aintree meeting, and it was he who introduced Edward William Topham, known as 'the Wizard' in tribute to his delicate skill as a handicapper which did so much to procure an exciting and equitably balanced contest. Topham became an important man in the organisation generally, beginning the Topham family's uninterrupted line of descent as the organising geniuses behind the Grand National.

Three more years passed. 'Discount' in 1844, 'Cure All' in 1845 —a brutal run this, over a deeply frozen track—and 'Pioneer' in 1846 were the winners. Gradually the race was developing its modern format, and next, in 1847, it was officially entitled the

Grand National for the first time. 'Matthew' won on this auspicious occasion. By this stage the course as well as the handicap steeplechase itself was moulded into a pattern destined to last over a hundred years. Flagging and trenching and other sophistications made the way over the ploughed lands more accessible for the contestants. The course became better marked and less cruel. It started at the grandstand, where Lynn's flat races had begun twenty years before and pursued a line to the first and longer brook, then it angled back when it met the Leeds–Liverpool Canal, establishing the well-known Canal Turn, and thus back over a second brook across the flat, back to the grandstand and round again.

The Grand National had arrived definitively as a great sporting and social occasion. The principal feature in its twelve-year growth to maturity was an increasing discipline, which it owed to men like Lynn, Bentinck, and Topham, who were the prime movers in urging for evermore precision and care in the presentation of the race, so that it was increasingly fairer as a contest and more viewable as a spectacle. This replacement of the haphazard and lawless ways of old was a reflection of the expanding discipline and orderliness slowly introduced into many sectors and aspects of Victorian life, not only in sport, but in law, administration, and so forth.

There is a disappointing side to this. In raising racing relatively quickly to this much higher standard, the management of the sport appeared to climb on to and remain on a plateau. Development has been comparatively static since. Racing is, by modern standards, a somewhat primitive sport, often with ramshackle amenities and inefficient communications, and more probably than in any other sport, the scope for shady activity remains a little too broad. Reasons for this perhaps include the exclusiveness of the sport at its higher levels and the practical effect of having many centres that are operational only very occasionally. Certainly, to stand this spring at Becher's or the Canal Turn would enable the spectator to watch, for better and for worse, much the same style and pattern as the 1847 Grand National.

Page 53 (*Above*) The 1839 Grand National—the first year the title was used;
(*below*) The start of the 1966 Grand National

in
ro-
his
he
ws
a l
en
y.
ose
ith
of
mi-
air-
ion

Sir
ch,
ved
ans,
the

Page 54 (*Left*) Michael
James Whitty, first Chief
Constable of Liverpool;
(*below*) Walton Prison,
opened 120 years ago and
still in full use

CHAPTER THREE

The inauguration of the Liverpool Police Force

A102 houses for the receipt of stolen goods, 2,071 resorts of thieves, 520 brothels, averaging 4 prostitutes in each, 625 resorts of ill-fame, 136 houses lodging prostitutes, 176 lodging-houses known to accommodate thieves, 55 taverns with brothels attached and 1,496 houses lodging known thieves; such was the extensive coverage of vice described by the Liverpool authorities in a Memorandum for the Constabulary Commission which reported in 1839. It suggested that over 5,000, or nearly 10 per cent, of Liverpool's buildings were engaged in vice and crime. It may well have been an exaggeration, but this is unlikely, for Liverpool was not anxious to be embroiled in the County Constabulary Act to which the 1839 Commission led. The borough police had been reformed in 1835, and the authorities now carefully watched over its operations. The Mayor of Liverpool defended the borough in stirring words, claiming it to be the most peaceful in the realm and one that had found no need of military intervention for many years. It is a moot point whether the Commission felt able to reconcile this mayoral eulogy with the foregoing description of the licentious welcome afforded visiting sailors on their nights ashore.

Far from being an exaggeration, one might even suggest that there were other brothel-keepers and saloon-owners laughing up their crooked sleeves at their ability to escape observation. Apart from these, there were 12,000 tap-rooms, beer-houses and the like, most of them open until well after midnight, while, as if to cater for a round-the-clock trade, a thousand of them reopened, even on Sundays, between four and six o'clock in the morning. Then there were the forty innocently labelled 'singing-rooms' of which John Clay, chaplain to Preston Gaol and a noted social commentator remarked: 'The evil wrought in such a singing-room in a single night outweighs all the good that can be effected by a dozen Sunday-schools in a year.'

With a plethora of shady dives and alcoholic premises for every hundred or so of the population, a heavy crime rate and atmosphere of social malaise was not unexpected. Liverpool had a mobile, roving population of thousands; sailors poured in from the docks and Irish immigrants arrived in their hundreds to a place where there was a relatively little staple industry to absorb them, and employment was normally casual and unskilled. They lived in conditions of utter deprivation, crowded and jostled together in an indescribable squalor. After London, Liverpool was the saddest example of industrialism and urbanisation creating a choking, swirling maelström of humanity, with which came an intensification and a reorientation of crime. As dockland expanded, theft and prostitution tightened their grasp, often with thief and whore working in evil concert. Canals and railways brought a not surprising rash of canal and railway robberies; 12,000 lads under fifteen, it was said, attempted to live by theft, their agile operations engineered by some 2,000 Merseyside Fagins. Away from the docks, Williamson Square was the leading vice-spot, with a score or more gambling and drinking saloons.

Most amazing of all, especially for those reared in the literary genre of unruly Cornwall and 'Jamaica Inn', Liverpool boasted the nation's leading wrecking area. At this time, shipping approached the port by way of the Rock Channel, tacking a line across the head of the Wirral peninsula, and where the pleasing suburban reaches of the Wirral now stand, the Liverpool wreckers lured many a ship to its doom. The females of the breed were no less dreadful than their consorts, and one of their tasks was to ransack the bodies of the crew. Should a ring prove obdurate, they thought nothing of biting off a sailor's finger or ear that they might remove its ornament at leisure. It was a perilous life for seamen, nearly ten thousand of whom might be in the port at any one time. They negotiated the hazards of wrecking only to be fastened upon by the thieves, tricksters, and street-women awaiting them at the docks. Perhaps there was something of a 'town and gown' feud. Years earlier, in 1775, 3,000 sailors had mutinied for higher pay, and ran riot throughout the town, looting, burning, and destroying, and in a bravura action guaranteed to make many a ratepayer's fingers itch, they hauled cannon ashore and bombarded the town hall. They were dispersed only by the arrival of troops.

This mutiny pointed to a further element of nineteenth-century disorder, the danger of mob action, bred in the cramped, grey anonymity of the large towns. Given its heritage of political militancy, Liverpool was strangely quiet during the Chartist uprisings of mid-nineteenth century. Many of the post-industrial campaigns and demonstrations were founded on solidarity about a given trade—the textile workers in Preston's 1842 Plug-plot riots or the St Helen's miners in their strike of 1831. Possibly the very crudity of Liverpool's labour mart, with its haphazard, drifting character, prevented considerable mass action, although Liverpool politicos and religionists were not averse to building up mobs to lend assistance to their varied objectives. The vigilante principle, quite widespread in eighteenth-century England, had sometimes to be implemented. At the north end of Toxteth Park, 20,000 impoverished and depraved beings were packed into squalid courts of houses erected by the Earl of Sefton, and their 'depredations' (to use the vogue-Victorianism) were such that the inhabitants of the wealthier southern side of Toxteth Park felt obliged to establish a private patrol to defend their property.

Property was sacrosanct. It was the mundane, day-by-day theft that troubled shopkeepers, merchants, and owner-occupiers of Liverpool. It was the constant sneak-thieving that irritated, not so much the occasional mob eruption that terrified, which proved to be the chief motive for police reform. That the terrible Victorian vice of drunkenness was in close alliance with this petty crime cannot be doubted. The *Liverpool Journal* of 28 March 1835 dolefully related how 'the Rev F. Murphy left the pulpit of St Patrick's, Toxteth Park, in tears after denouncing the disgraceful scenes of riot and drunkenness on St Patrick's Day'. Both his patron and his parochial saint had been abused, and, with gin selling at eight shillings a gallon at every corner, the drab duo of drink and theft cast a seamy gloom over the entire borough.

Any catalogue of Merseyside crime underlines the point. The large-scale public disorder which is frequently used to explain police reform was rarely found in Liverpool, and few, if any, punishments for riot or other avowedly political misdemeanours are recorded. Police reorganisation predated the major Victorian mass movements such as Chartism, while, as an incident as late as the Liverpool Police Strike of 1919 was aptly to demonstrate, army and even navy were still to be required in the event of massive disturbance.

It has been possible to extract from the national archives the names of those men, convicted in Liverpool, who were serving sentences as attested convicts in the last quarter of 1838. At this time, convicts whose crimes demanded the severe reproach of commitment at national level were earmarked for transportation, but one of the by-products of the colonists' victory in the American War of Independence had been the halting of this traffic. As a stopgap the notorious 'hulks', well known to readers of *Great Expectations*, were established, and more and more of the transportees were drafted eastward to New South Wales. Eight such 'hulks' existed in 1838, three of them anchored, not off the east coast fens, but at St Georges, Bermuda, although incarceration below decks in the West Indian climate must have been unwholesome in the extreme. Lawrence Johnson was serving a seven-year term on the *York* at Portsmouth, and four from Liverpool, all under twenty-one, were out in the West Indies, on the *Antelope*, the *Dromedary* and the *Coromandel*. For stealing a knife or a pair of candlesticks, their sentences ranged from seven to fourteen years. No less than thirty-seven men convicted at Liverpool or Kirkdale were to be found on the *Fortitude* at Chatham. During the last quarter of 1838, fourteen were dispatched to New South Wales and one, more happily, was pardoned. Seven years was the most lenient sentence. Twenty-one-year-old Robert Black was transported for life for housebreaking, and thirty-year-old Sam Weston for stealing a horse and cart. Many received fourteen-year sentences for what appear to be trifling offences, although, of course, the lists say nothing of previous record. Andrew Frazer, aged nineteen, was sentenced to fourteen years for stealing 4s 6d, while Joe Case, a year younger, and Tom Downs, just over twenty years of age, received similar sentences for taking two pairs of shoes and a leg of mutton respectively.

The *Ganymede* at Woolwich housed another twenty-four of Liverpool's miscreants, nineteen of whom joined shipments to New South Wales during the quarter in question—Thomas Whittaker for life, having been convicted of stealing a mare. During the same period Henry Pike, aged twenty-one, serving a fourteen-year sentence for stealing twenty-seven sovereigns, died of 'a brain affection'. Fourteen more Liverpool convicts were imprisoned on the *Justitia*, also at Woolwich, all of them serving terms of from ten to fifteen years for theft, including Thomas Jones, just seventeen, who received fourteen years for stealing a watch.

Most tragic of all was the *Euryalus* at Chatham. Here lay the juvenile offenders, nine of them from Liverpool: Peter Burns, aged sixteen, seven years for stealing a pair of boots; Pat Conway, aged fourteen, fourteen years for stealing money; William Morton, a fourteen-year-old consumptive, seven years for 'larceny by a servant'; and three sixteen-year-olds—Patrick Tute, George Williams, and James Edwards—all with ten-year sentences for theft. Lastly, there were two 'lifers': Matthew Carlisle, a fifteen-year-old housebreaker, and William Naylor, a thirteen-year-old who had stolen a cow. The calendar is as dismal as it is repetitive, and, later in the century, Liverpool itself was to take up the juvenile 'hulk' notion when the Akbar Float Brigade Reformatory was docked in the Mersey estuary.

In all, eighty-nine Liverpolitan criminals were at that particular stroke of time awaiting or undergoing transportation. Only five assault cases broke the even tenor of theft as the single crime leading to national commitment. A further delving into the attested lists demonstrates that this pattern continued to be a constant one. The ferocity of the punishments recalls that, despite the new disappearance of the death-penalty, and the purportedly rationalised legal reforms associated with Sir Robert Peel, the gigantic crime-wave of early Victorian England was met by brutal, stiff sentences and nothing more.

These criminals are shadowy figures, and the image of a thirteen-year-old boy stealing a cow and being incarcerated for life offers only the outline of a tragic tale. In an effort, however, to build up a case for police reform, the Constabulary Commission, established in the 1830s, prepared a questionnaire to be completed by police officials and prison governors in regard of representative prisoners in their charge. These documents, tied by musty pink ribbon in bundles in the Public Record Office, amount to brief, formal biographies of the criminally inclined. Luckily, Mr Bachelor, governor of Liverpool's central bridewell, was an assiduous correspondent with the Constabulary Commission and a diligent interviewer when armed with their *pro forma* of questions. Of the thirty-two concerned with prisoners in Lancashire, twenty-four are the proud work of Mr Bachelor, and they provide neat pen-pictures of what otherwise would be mere names. One example must suffice.

John Edwards was a Liverpool youth of fifteen, awaiting trial for taking a drawer containing money out of a shop. He had been working two and a half years, initially in a druggist's shop and later in the employ of a copperplate fitter. He was illegitimate, but both his parents were living, and he had lived with them. His father, described as 'honest, industrious and sober', was self-employed as an auctioneer and appraiser, although the terms may well have been a trifle ostentatious, while John's mother had left to live with another man some two years previously. His father was often absent on business, none the less, 'great care' had been taken of him; he had attended day school and night school over a ten-year period; he was literate and had been a regular churchgoer. The only traumatic experience related was when, after being 'induced' to run away from home by other boys, he had been tied to a bedpost and flogged.

Surprisingly, it was the 'bad companions' he fell in with under the sober auspices of night school that set him on the primrose path. He stopped reading the Bible and attending service, and he confessed to participating in forty 'depredations'. He had been 'apprehended' six times and convicted five times, and four shillings was, pathetically, his grandest weekly haul. He had used pawn-brokers as receivers. There were seventy-one questions posed in all, many attempting to lead the questioner into blaming the system: 'Did you derive encouragement in your criminal courses from the remissness of the police or constables?' was such a one. Police reformers favoured a 'preventive' police designed so thoroughly to permeate society that crime would virtually reach a standstill. This was why cases like those of John Edwards were significant, for, ostensibly, his was not a deprived background; it was, so the argument ran, insufficient 'fear of constables' that had caused the trouble. Bachelor himself forwarded a memorandum to the commission on juvenile delinquency in which he blamed the 'facilities existing for depredation', and he spoke of children, one ten and one nine years old, serving short sentences in his gaol.

It was against this canvas of lawlessness that police reform was attempted. Expanding criminality, bred of the industrial and urban boom, had overrun the rickety outmoded devices of yester-year, with only a brutal judiciary, striking harshly and hap-hazardly, to defend society. In September 1835 the Municipal In-corporations Act was passed. Three months later the first elec-tions were held with the enlarged franchise, and, as if to confirm the old council's reluctance to accept the new statute, only two of its number were re-elected, and the Liberals romped home gaining 43 out of the 48 seats.

Policing was, in practice, the only novel function introduced by the 1835 Act into Liverpool, and no time was lost. At the first reformed council meeting a watch committee of twenty-four was formed, this being obligatory under the new legislation. Under the chairmanship of John Holmes the watch committee met on 16 January 1836, and immediately a sub-committee was appointed to investigate the existing position. One superintendent, 44 con-stables and 17 supernumeraries formed a day force, although, in spite of 'so large an expenditure' as £8,000 per annum, it was 'not employed as a preventive force, being chiefly engaged in the apprehension of felons, the service of warrants and summonses, attendance on magistrates, and at the daily sessional courts'. There was 'no permanent street patrol', and six of the constables re-mained all day long at St George's Pier. A further £3,400 was spent on the 'singularly defective' policing of the extra-parochial districts of Toxteth Park, Low Hill, Edge Hill, Everton, and Kirkdale.

Then there were the night watchmen. They consisted of 1 superintendent, 16 captains and 150 watchmen and orderlies, 45 of them 'unfit' and 25 with 'very doubtful' qualifications. They cost £9,200 each year, so that over £20,000 was expended in a wellnigh fruitless exercise. The night watch had remained an ineffective body, despite the attempts of several superintendents to revitalise it. Mr Parlow, late of the Metropolitan Police was one, and his successor John Shipp was another. Shipp had enjoyed a chequered career; he had absconded from a Suffolk poorhouse and enlisted in the army, from which he was twice discharged, only for Colonel Rowan, the Metropolitan Police Commissioner, to offer him an inspectorship. He followed Parlow to Liverpool, wrote a farce that was performed at the Theatre Royal and later became governor of Liverpool Workhouse. His funeral was at-tended by a massive turnout of Liverpool's paupers. But his endeavours had been in vain; in the last year of the watch as many as 61 were dismissed, ranging from 39 discharged for inebriation to the solitary soul who had established 'improper connection with a female prisoner'.

Since 1811 there had also been a dock police. By 1835 it engaged a superintendent—the zealous Mr Dowling, who had reported to the Constabulary Commission on wreckers—4 very busy inspectors, 12 sergeants and 138 privates, all at a cost of £8,000 a year. This para-military outfit was the most efficient of Liverpool's three arms of the law, and it is significant that the most successful force was the one entirely recruited for the safety of merchandise.

The watch committee took a stong line on reform. It is now often argued that the Benthamite influence was not as potent in social reform as once was thought, and that 'intolerability' led to piecemeal renovation. But Liverpool's Liberal watch committee maintained a doctrinaire approach, in part influenced by the London pattern and in part seeming to quote literally the views of Edwin Chadwick, the key member of the Constabulary Commission just about to be appointed and the leading exponent of police reform in the Benthamite school. Their 'ultimate object was the establishment of an efficient preventive police' based upon a plan which 'with little addition to the sum expended upon a system which has been found to be totally inadequate might by diminishing crime, prove a saving in contingent expenses'. Although other formulas were at hand, the committee plumped directly for the preventive principle, founded as it was on economic rather than on moral bases. They called for a single constabulary under a head constable, with 4 superintendents, 24 inspectors ('so removed in point of class' to avoid 'undue familiarity' with the men) and nearly 300 permanent constables. 'The expenses, in wages and clothes, of an effective and well-organised constabulary force' would be £24,000, and it would be a vast improvement on the existing 'vicious system'. The head constable was to receive £450 and each superintendent £150 in salary, with inspectors on 30s and constables on 18s per week.

The borough was divided into two divisions, with the dividing line running from the foot of Water Street, by the waterfront, along Dale Street and Shaw's Brow to Low Hill. The central office and bridewell was to remain at the existing premises in Exchange Street East, and the night-watch superintendent, John

Michael Whitty, was appointed Liverpool's first head constable.

It had been suggested that a 'fearless course of removal' be applied to the existing force, as 'few of its members will be found eligible for reappointment'. Nevertheless, 53 of the night watch alone were sworn in, along with 61 other applicants, some of them from the borough or extra-parochial day watches. Twelve of the inspectors were also recruited from among the captains of existing forces. This is not surprising. On paper, the police was new, but who but the serving constables and watchmen had the experience or the desire to work long hours in dangerous conditions under stringent rules for 18s weekly? So low a wage meant recruitment from the lower orders, where the 'blue butchers' were most suspected. By the end of February, however, 324 men had been appointed.

The Metropolitan Police was naturally the model, and its commissioner, Richard Wayne, advised the watch committee on certain matters. The military flavour was to be noted. Two of the four superintendents were retired army lieutenants, and the administrative format of two divisions, each with two sets of four sections divided into beats, was based on the infantry regiment. Uniforms of top hat, frock coat and trousers, and considerable foot-drill added to the martial tinge, and, less it be thought the truncheon was felt to be more humane than the musket, it was Chadwick's viewpoint that the baton, by leaving a free hand, made 'apprehension' the simpler. The Castle Museum at York has an original Liverpool specimen in its splendid display of truncheons; it is a stern-looking stick, perhaps a foot only in length, but of an intimidating shape, and bearing the royal insignia and the borough monogram.

It was not until the summer of 1837 that the dock police amalgamated with the borough force, and Dowling became Whitty's deputy. The watch committee hoped that this would end the 'constant bickerings and jealousies between the two police forces, arising from supposed acts of mutual interference', for apart from these wrangles, the borough police had not enjoyed an enthusiastic reception from the press. *The Liverpool Mail* spoke in November 1836 of 'an increase of remorseless, invidious and unpardonable oppression' and 'no diminution of crime' whatsoever. Even the Liberal *Liverpool Mercury* was critical. In March 1836 the *Mercury* felt that violence 'was resorted to rather too often, and that if the practice be not checked some of the new police may find, to their cost, that they will not be able to make free with the heads and limbs of His Majesty's subjects with impunity'.

The policemen may well have read this ruefully. The *Liverpool Mercury* frequently published accounts of injuries to the police; in April 1836 a crowd in Vauxhall Road attempted to release some prisoners and badly mauled their police escort; in May, PC Dwyer was stabbed by a sixteen-year-old girl; in June, Inspector Martin was assaulted and locked in a cellar by William Langden and it required twelve colleagues to release him; and in July, Inspector Barry and some of his men were burned severely by three desperadoes. So the catalogue continued month by month, and on top of this the magistracy were not over-sympathetically inclined towards the police, and complaints of false accusation were also showered upon them.

The annual report of the watch committee in 1838 was the first survey of a full year at full strength. It was a mixed report. There was enthusiasm for the deterrent nature of prevention, as the 'presence and vigilance' of the police had made for comparative good order. Of 2,480 thieves arrested, 2,391 were apprehended under suspicion of being 'about to commit a felony', and 4,817 of the 7,653 felons arrested were taken at or just after the offence. The public were encouraged to co-operate in the preventive approach by the news that 5,343 out of 5,847 informations laid had led to convictions. 'Constant vigilance', said the report, harries criminals into 'a state of harassing uncertainty'. On the debit side, costs had doubled on the original estimate and stood now at £50,000. Many men had proved unreliable, partly because 'several worthless individuals' had been accepted. The complement was now 574. In 1838, 175 had left, of whom 101 had been dismissed. As many as 876 dismissals, fines, and reprimands had been recorded in the year, including 282 for inebriation. This reflected the national picture, and it was not only in the pursuit of 'ardent spirits' that the policeman vied with the criminal; the drunken constable, hunched long hours over his lonely tankard, was throughout the land the consequence of ostracism within his own social grouping.

Over the next twenty years the pattern remained fairly constant. The over-optimistic enthusiasts for the 'preventive' theory had their more naïve hopes dashed, in that crime showed few signs of abating. Indeed, the purist view was soon abandoned. In 1844, only two years after the famous CID commenced its exploits, Liverpool began a detective force of eight men, which by 1860 had grown to twenty-two. The positive role of the police, after the commission of a crime, began to supersede a little the original negative tack of prevention. Perhaps the public appetite for that favourite Victorian byline, 'melancholy incident', contributed to this in psychological fashion. Cure was and is more spectacular than prevention, and the Chadwickian deterrent theory soon faded into the background.

The force had its troubles. Four chief constables were in office over those first twenty years, and several committees of inquiry were appointed to examine varied aspects of police-work. Clashes with the magistrates continued throughout the period, and indiscipline remained rife. There were 2,674 disciplinary reports against constables in 1842, and in 1847, there were 224 constables charged with being drunk on duty and—a subtle distinction—347 charged with being the worse for liquor. The lawless milieu was unchanging. There was one beer-house or public-house to every 162 of the population and nearly 600 brothels in the early 1850s. Niggling petty theft proved still the constant irritation, and the police dealt annually with over 20,000 offences, the great majority of them small-scale crimes of gain. There were signs that the police were being accepted, albeit grudgingly. Their work in the suppression of mob violence and their heroic labours in times of distress, such as in the dreadful aftermath left by the hurricane of January 1839, induced the populace to think a little more kindly of them.

The Police Act of 1856 obliged all boroughs and counties to form a police force, and subjected it to an annual inspection upon which state grants depended. The first chief constable of Lancashire, Sir John Woodford, became the first Inspector of Constabulary for the North, and he found the Liverpool police 'in a most complete and satisfactory state of efficiency and discipline'. There were now 886 officers, and the ratio to population of one to 445 was bettered only by the Metropolitan Police. H. Shimmins, writing articles on 'Liverpool Life' in the *Liverpool Mercury* in 1855, described the Liverpool police as 'the model force of the country', a judgement confirmed by Woodford, who spoke of 'the great numerical strength of this establishment and the high degree of efficiency in which it is constantly maintained'.

This repute was hard won, and it is a trifle churlish to place it in perspective. The abysmal condition of other forces and the obvious comparison with what Shimmins called the 'veritable Dogberries' of the pre-1835 days threw the new police into a favourable light, and again, the stress of sheer necessity bore hard on a crowded cosmopolitan port—Liverpool had to have a more effective police force than practically anywhere else.

So began the long history of the modern police in Liverpool. Alongside this development, the penal system was also evolving steadily. In 1855 Walton gaol was opened to replace the borough gaol in Great Howard Street. The local lock-ups were fast becoming inadequate for the needs of ever-growing conurbations, and transportation was slowly disappearing. Instead, a network of national prisons was established, most of them modelled on the radical 'starfish' design of Pentonville. Walton, at a cost of nearly £200,000 was one of these, mapped out on the Benthamite thesis of economically planned observation controls over a 'separate and silent system' of about a thousand single cells. Soon 300 hammocks had to be added, as the governor William Jameson led his staff of 55 'dicipline officers' and 33 other officials in the rigid observation of their strictly imposed regulations. Cellular isolation, and the unremitting monotony of penal labour, was sterile and clinical when compared with the slapdash free-for-all of earlier prison styles, but it was arduous and depressing beyond measure and it is small wonder that little Joseph Davies, aged twelve, attempted suicide in the opening months of the prison's story. And Walton still stands today, some miles from the centre of Liverpool, its system manifestly more civilised and humane than at its inception, but a sombre and forbidding Victorian edifice for all that.

Some knowledge of the beginnings of the police and prison service helps an understanding of contemporary problems, for despite obvious and welcome changes, the administrative format for both is very much the same. There may also be some cold comfort in the knowledge that the present so-called crime wave is by no means a novelty.

CHAPTER FOUR

Liverpool and the new Poor Law

Liverpool sadly bears out the scriptural maxim of the abiding presence of the poor. In 1794, according to the Liverpool historian, Ramsey Muir, there was 'so large a population living on the verge of penury and in conditions which encouraged thriftlessness', that one-fortieth of the populace found themselves in the workhouse. Poor relief was administered then, as it had been from Elizabethan times, by the parish. Each Easter the rate-payers adjourned to St Nicholas Church to elect churchwardens and overseers, and a committee of these supervised the collection of poor-rates and their disbursement. Poor relief in Liverpool was, said Muir, 'perhaps better administered than anywhere else in England', and it certainly compared favourably, as the Liverpool clergy doubtless enjoyed pointing out, with the riotous confusion of the Manchester Poor Law in the late eighteenth century. During the French wars, and under the influence of Dr Roscoe, poor relief was handled sensibly in Liverpool, and despite some dreadful extravagances in the 1820s, this reputation was maintained. W. L. Blease, the historian of Liverpool's old Poor Law, spoke proudly of its reputation. The Liverpool Select Vestry appointed under the Sturges Bourne Act of 1784 came, he said, to be noted for its 'purity and economy in the conduct of public business' and 'few townships of that day could point to a more blameless history', with its 'lively spirit of enterprise' and 'enlightened sense of public duty'.

In the many years following the Napoleonic Wars, however, there were many, in Liverpool as elsewhere, ready to criticise the principle of relief at base. The leading critic in Liverpool was Henry Booth, the author, in 1824, of the pamphlet *Thoughts on the Condition of the Poor in Large Towns, especially with Reference to Liverpool*. He acknowledged the sound practice of the select vestry, but, in strict laissez-faire terms, he propounded that 'any artificial system which shall provide subsistence, independently of such profitable employment, will actually create the recipients of its own bounty'. He mainly blamed, after Malthus, 'the super-abundance of labour, compared with the labour to be performed' and conjectured that full employment was 'delusive'. This situation was exacerbated by taxation, tithes, corn laws and other anti-private fiscal devices which Booth felt led to a decline in commerce. The country, he also argued, placed surplus hands in the large towns, where even the normal individual 'ventures in a lottery'. And then the actions directed against such poverty 'relax the exertions of the labouring classes, by holding out the prospect of a maintenance, independent of their own efforts, thereby preventing that activity, economy and forethought, which we should promote as essential ingredients in the characters of the working classes of society'. To ram home the point, he alluded to the sixty licensed and the numberless unlicensed pawnbrokers of Liverpool. 'Some of the profession have retired with a handsome competency and even keep their carriages.' He calculated that £9,000 per year was made by some pawnbrokers from 'the privations and guilt of the poorest classes'. Even in the 1820s, Booth was prepared to estimate that of these 'poorest classes' who were keeping the pawnbrokers in such princely style, two-thirds were Irish.

This was the orthodox Benthamite view of the day. While untutored in the subtleties of Benthamism, there were many rate-payers prepared to lend an approximate support to that credo as the poor-rate soared to a national average of £6 or £7 millions in the early thirties. There must, argued Chadwick, Nassau Senior, and their kind, be a free trade in labour as in commerce. Labour, rather than be synthetically sustained by parochial doles, must be forced on to a free and open mart. Hence the stern principle of 'less-eligibility', with 'the workhouse test' providing that indoor relief would be materially 'less-eligible' than the lowest form of working life. Outdoor relief was to be abolished, and, given a daunting workhouse system, the labour force would be compelled to turn its hand to anything. This briefly is the explanation of the unrelenting image of the Victorian workhouse. If Oliver Twist were given more, he might find the workhouse preferable to an available job.

'Less-eligibility', coupled with a rational and economic organisation, was the keynote of the 1834 Poor Law Amendment Act, a major and seminal reform that was the basis of the national welfare scheme until 1929. Before the passage of the act, a Royal Commission collected an enormous bulk of evidence on the existing Poor Law, and among the manifold volumes was Report Number 21 by Gilbert Henderson on the County Palatine of Lancaster. He received a vast number of answers to a questionnaire completed by a wide sample of urban and rural areas, and he included a series of individual accounts of various towns in his report, from which a valuable picture of Liverpool's Poor Law system, on the eve of reform, may be drawn.

Liverpool's population was 165,000 in 1831, a rise of 46,000 since the 1821 census. In the same period, the annual expenditure had risen not alarmingly from £33,700 to £34,500; indeed, the per capita expense had dropped from 5s 8d to 4s 2d. A Select Vestry of twenty controlled poor relief. There were 1,661 in the workhouse, almost exactly 1 per cent of the population, of whom 426 were put to work of a tedious and unprofitable nature. That segregation of classes of paupers so dear to the hearts of ardent reformers was 'not completed in Liverpool', but the weekly cost of keeping a pauper—3s 2d—was in keeping with their reforming zeal. Much of the service was casual relief for the Irish, but 'home visits' were made as frequently as possible to ensure an efficient scheme was maintained.

The existing structure of the Select Vestry had been in train since 1821 and had proved 'beneficial' to the town. Six of the twenty overseers who made up the Select Vestry committee were engaged in business, usually of a mercantile kind, while quite a troupe of officers were in full-time employ. There were five assistant overseers, who conducted inquiries into applications for relief, a treasurer, a secretary, a 'payer-out', a 'bastardy' officer and the workhouse governor, as well as a number of clerks and eight rate collectors. It was the Select Vestry which made the actual decision as to the amount of money annually to be raised.

Henderson made specific mention of Liverpool in his report, and his comments helpfully eke out the normal responses to the urban questionnaire. He confirmed the view held then and since on the success of the Poor Law service. 'Liverpool affords a striking example of the operation of a Select Vestry under Mr Sturges Bourne's act in reducing the parish expenditure.' In the last year before the Select Vestry was appointed, expenditure per

head had been 7s 9½d. In 1831 it was 4s 2d. This represented a
saving of £27,000 at a time when national expenditure was ex-
orbitantly high and the per capita cost had jumped nearly to 10s.
'By a thorough investigation of all these cases', the number of
outdoor-paupers had dropped from 3,222 to 1,435 and of indoor-
paupers (that is, resident in the workhouse as opposed to receiving
hand-outs at home) from 1,492 to 1,009 in the same period. 'Great
exertions were also made to provide work' of a manual kind—
road-work, digging fields and so on—and 'many under this system
who had been for years in the workhouse, quitted it and eventually found employment for themselves elsewhere'.

A stricter management had led to the enhancing of Liverpool's
already good repute for Poor Law control. Five boards of four
overseers sat each morning in rotation, with the salaried secretary
playing a 'leading part' and ensuring continuity. Henderson
watched 250 cases dealt with by such a board on such a morning,
and most were refused. He was impressed by the stiffness of the
procedure and the standard of report produced by the assistant
overseer after his visit to the applicant's home, if he had one. The
Irish applied in crowds, requesting 'to be relieved and passed to
Dublin'. In the financial year 1832–3, 2,975 Irish had made such a
claim, and, although Gilbert Henderson recognised their 'poverty
and wretchedness', he was prepared to condemn many of them
roundly as liars.

'The workhouse is frequently used', he reported, 'as a test for
the real necessities of applicants for relief.' It was the nation's
largest, with room for 1,750 and almost full to capacity during
Henderson's visit. The governor had introduced paid door-
keepers, separation of the sexes, and oakum-picking, the last providing an excellent working model of 'less-eligibility'. Oakum
'thinned the house very much', but when it was in scanty supply,
'paupers flocked in'; 'a load of junk before the door would deter
them for a long time'. There was educational and some industrial
work for children, and apprenticeships were occasionally
arranged. The paupers were 'in constant confinement, except for
a few hours every month', a liberty that was normally enjoyed on
a Thursday evening, and in his only criticism of Liverpool, Henderson severely pronounced that this was abused 'to the scandal
of the establishment'. It should be perhaps explained that the
sexes were segregated, including husbands and wives, not only

Page 71   The Liverpool Poor House, about 1770

Page 72   The latest old people's homes, Leighton Dene, Liverpool

to add to the austere regimen, but to avoid the generation of further paupers, to say nothing of the added burdens for the 'bastardy' officer. Gilbert Henderson was alarmed by Thursday's lack of inhibitions. Certainly there were lock-wards for each sex, and no more than twenty 'able-bodied paupers' were resident in the workhouse.

The fever hospital held 140. Because of the generous use of chloride of lime and whitewash, cholera victims over the last ten years had been no more than ten, with four fatalities. This was a remarkably low figure, considering the comings and goings of hundreds of paupers, but, of course, the chief cholera epidemics still lay dolefully in the future. All in all, Gilbert Henderson was encouraged by most of what he saw, and given the Irish inundations and the heavy rate of unemployment, he doubted 'whether the advantage of the poorer classes would be promoted by any relaxation'.

It was ostensibly on the basis of such reports that the Poor Law Amendment Act was passed. Mark Blaug, having recently studied these reports, claims that they were not scrutinised thoroughly by the reformers, and that their testimony did not support the case against an extravagant and artificial system of relief. After 1834 the newly formed Poor Law Commission, with its headquarters at Somerset House, began to rationalise relief procedures. Assistant Poor Law Commissioners toured the country, grouping parishes into unions which were to be controlled by elected boards of guardians. Their task was to supervise relief locally under the guidance and inspection of the central body. The massive resistance to this movement is well known and has, in the case of Lancashire, been frequently exaggerated. The press certainly entered into the controversy in a lively manner. In Liverpool, the Whig *Liverpool Mercury* supported and the Tory *Liverpool Courier* opposed the new law; the former desired to underline the brutishness of the opposition and the latter to emphasise its force. Together they succeeded in giving a larger than life view of the actual objections. None the less, there was active opposition—from the working classes rightly suspicious of the temper of the reform to the Tories and extreme radicals who distrusted the centralising tendencies of Somerset House. There were many strands in the opposition, but one significant one has sometimes been overlooked. Simply, in some areas of which

Liverpool was one, there was not much wrong with the existing system, assessing it on the Poor Law Commission's own terms. There was an elected committee, a well-run workhouse, full-time officers and sound financial supervision. There was everything the commission desired except its own central powers, and these were to prove feeble over the early years.

In brief, the national expenditure per head on poor relief in 1833 was 9s 9d. In Liverpool it was little more than 4s. In assessments of opposition to the new poor law this feature has sometimes been omitted. Along with bourgeois fears of central interference, working-class suspicions of the severity of the measure, parochial resentment at loss of independence and the dozen other objections, there was also the valid opinion that little was wrong with the old régime. Thus in Liverpool, as in other Lancastrian towns, people objected to the Whig Poor Law reform not because they disliked its tenets, but because they believed they already acted upon them.

In a letter to the *Liverpool Mercury* in 1836, T. Frankland Lewis, one of the three Poor Law Commissioners, warned that 'the Assistant Poor Law Commissioner will shortly proceed into Lancashire'. In this case the Assistant Poor Law Commissioner was Alfred Power, a friend of Edwin Chadwick and an enthusiastic Benthamite lawyer. He worked with speed, zest and skill to 'unionise' the county, and through the winter of 1836–7, he made a clean sweep of Lancashire except for the Lunesdale district, Lancaster, Salford, Manchester, and Liverpool. Soon Lancaster, Manchester, and Salford had been organised into unions, leaving only Liverpool and the Lunesdale district of seventeen parishes already unified as the Caton Incorporation for Poor Law purposes. It was not until March 1841, seven years after the Act, that the Poor Law Commission dealt with Liverpool and established the Liverpool Poor Law Union.

The story may be traced in the Liverpool Parish Records. A general meeting was called for 11 March 1841 to consider 'such measures as may prevent the introduction of the New Poor Law into this parish'. A day or so later a Special General Vestry was summoned and vainly resolved 'that considering the satisfactory manner in which the present system has been managed in Liverpool, this meeting strongly deprecates so great an alteration'. In spite of this strenuous opposition, which had kept at bay the new law for seven years, the Poor Law Commission was determined to go ahead. On 20 March Liverpool's returning officer, Henry Lawrence, was asked to arrange the election of a Board of Guardians.

In its edition of 16 April the Whig *Liverpool Mercury* rejoiced to report the last Easter Vestry Meeting, applauding Mr Bryden, who said at the meeting that £239 spent by the Tories on opposition to the new Poor Law was 'a waste of parish money'. But in an advertisement the Tory Overseers expressed the hope that 'the feelings and wishes of the great body of rate-payers . . . will have their due weight'.

The Tories, however, proved highly adaptable. On 25 March James Aspinall, one of their number, nominated twenty-five names. Oddly there were no other nominations, so his twenty-five placemen were elected. Not content with this, the Parish Vestry had already placed a bill before Parliament for the repeal of the new system in Liverpool. The law was a dead letter before it was implemented. The Reverend A. Campbell was chairman both of Vestry and Board; nearly half the Guardians had been Select Vestrymen; E. Gray and J. Evans, the Vestry rate-collectors, were maintained as Assistant Overseers. A man called Rowlands, 'who', according to the *Mercury*, 'has rendered himself somewhat notorious in electioneering' was made a Relieving Officer for the poor. He was one of several 'out and out partisans' offered jobs, and he had in fact been tried but acquitted of an electoral offence.

To the *Mercury*'s chagrin, the Tory Guardians blatantly took yet another scarcely impartial step. The registration of births, deaths and marriages was the responsibility of the Poor Law Commission. Its headquarters at Somerset House is still, of course, the home of the Registrar-General, and many Poor Law premises, on Merseyside as elsewhere, still house present-day registraries. Where no Guardians existed to appoint local registrars, the central Poor Law Commission undertook to do so. In May of 1841, J. Boardman, the Superintendent Registrar appointed by the commission, was sacked for not 'passing muster with the Tories', according to the Whig *Mercury*. James Eckersley, who had been secretary to the Select Vestry, was given the job, and the link between old and new was even more solidly soldered. He was, pointed out the *Liverpool Mercury*, 'an illiterate person . . . a turncoat in religion and an apostate in politics'. The newspaper decided that 'the Tory Guardians have played a very dirty trick'. Eckersley was also appointed to the post of Clerk to the Union.

Still the Guardians were not satisfied. It was, no doubt, an irritating case of so near and yet so far from complete independence. Apart from changes in nomenclature, the only innovation was central inspection. By this time Power had transferred to Malvern, and Charles Mott was regional Assistant Commissioner. He obviously annoyed the Guardians a great deal, but at this distance it is uncertain how much of this was personal and how much simply the office he held. There were anomalies. The title 'union' was a misnomer, for Liverpool was the only 'union' in the country which consisted of a single parish, that is, it was in union with no one. Even so it was the largest Poor Law unit in the United Kingdom with, by now, 223,000 inhabitants.

The Tories were manifestly impatient. At a Special General Vestry in November 1841, it was resolved that 'it is the decided opinion of this Vestry after the experience they have had of the working of the new Poor Law that it is not wanted in this Parish, but that the system is more cumbersome and expensive, and is not so efficient or satisfactory either to the rich or poor as the Select Vestry system'. Application for a local act was vigorously pursued. James Aspinall, speaking at this parochial meeting in favour of a local Act, declared 'we don't know whether we act legally or not—we are so completely under the power of the deputy poor law commissioner, Mr Mott'. The case was mooted of 167 immigrants, presumably Irish, whom Mott insisted on being thrown in the workhouse, whereas the Liverpool practice was the cheaper one of resettling them for £300. This amounted to £20 provisions and the sea fares home. The Guardians were annoyed at Mott's dislike for this Powellite policy of repatriation, and they made much of Charles Mott's purportedly protracted and obsessive questioning of an item costing 6s.

The union had hardly operated six months. The Tories, however, were cockahoop at this time. Nationally, they had recuperated somewhat under the far-sighted leadership of Robert Peel. The Poor Law Commission had itself been emasculated by the departure of its keenest supporter, Edwin Chadwick, and it had lost much of its early doctrinaire vigour. Locally, the Tories had swept the board at the recent corporation elections, after a period of liberal municipal government subsequent to the Municipal

Reform Act of 1835. In allegiance with the Anglican church, which had a most extreme wing in Liverpool, the Tories were firmly in command. They were anxious to snap the tenuous line that held them to the central Poor Law agency. At the Easter Vestry in March 1842 a motion was carried regretting that the Vestry had 'no voice or discretion' in Poor Law administration. In pragmatic terms it was a lie, for so many guardians were Vestrymen and the supporters of the Vestry position.

The controversy over Liverpool's Poor Law autonomy is summarised in a Parliamentary Paper of 1842 entitled *Report on the Grounds of Exemption for Liverpool from the Poor Law Amendment Act*. It includes a bitter attack on the new Poor Law, which Eckersley, secretary to the Select Vestry and clerk to the Guardians, could not identify. It claimed that the parish administration had been sound, and, considering the numbers of casual poor, the rate of outdoor relief was low. There was a large workhouse holding nearly two thousand and, between 1836 and 1840, the average rate-levies had been no more than 1s 5d per head. The parochial organisation was preferable to 'a heterogeneous mass of duties' devolved on the clerk to the Board of Guardians, and various economies, connected with rationalising the assessment and collection of the poor rate, had been spoilt by the new Poor Law. Charles Mott was particularly blamed for this and it was said he kept 'the parish in constant turmoil'.

Faced with this anonymous memorandum, Mott counter-attacked fiercely. He said the document was factually incorrect and showed a basic misunderstanding of the Act. The workhouse accommodation was inadequate, the Select Vestry was an expensive organisation, there was insufficient vigilance with the casual paupers and the rate collection was inefficient. Mott made somewhat facile play of the 'many expressions of satisfaction' accorded the fact that the Superintendent Registrar was a dissenter 'whilst the present clerk to the Guardians was a member of the Church of England'. This fortuitous arrangement, he felt, reconciled the clergy.

The third section of the report was compiled by the churchwarden and overseers of the parish. They made some technical claims to exemption from the Poor Law Amendment Act on the grounds of certain prior local legislation, while, more practically, they reiterated the point that, with such a turnover of passing paupers, the rate was notably small. The rationalisation of rate-assessment, mentioned in the earlier and unsigned report, re-volved around the increase of population outpacing the spread of property with a consequent imbalance of inhabitants and rateable value. Mott had argued, it was claimed, that no funds existed for such an exercise, and he was further criticised for increasing expense by £330 through the employment of extra staff. The Guardians met less, stated the parish officers, than the Vestry had, and managerial standards had declined. For twenty years parochial affairs had been 'vigilantly and economically managed' and, as a final accolade, no less a personage than Sir Robert Peel had commented favourably on Liverpool's parochial governance.

This tended to sweep Mott's feeble protestations aside, and all his superiors at the Poor Law Commission could offer was a plaintive note that the commissioners 'have had no serious obstacle to contend with in the formation' of unions in very large towns such as Manchester. The Liverpool protagonists were steadfastly making the point that can be noticed, in a minor key, in other parts of Lancashire. The rigid uniformity of the system tended to steamroller beneficial local aberrations, such as Liverpool's proposed new look at the poor rate. The conservation of the parish was another feature. As so often happens in English local government, the new did not replace the old; the one merely added itself to the other. Thus in Liverpool and certainly throughout Lancashire, as Alfred Power was quick to note, the proposed rational use of experts broke down in that they were additions to the bureaucratic machine. It cannot be doubted that the Liverpool churchmen and Tories had a particular animus against Charles Mott, and whether this was a direct personality clash or whether he personified a hated system can hardly now be judged, but locally and nationally he was subjected to severe criticism.

The influence of the parish both on and outside the Board of Guardians was immense, and the government swiftly bowed to Liverpool's desire for independence. Because of its size, its cosmopolitan nature, and its character as a bustling seaport, it was determined that Liverpool should, as it were, go free. On the 30 June 1842, an Act for the Administration of the Laws relating to the Poor in the Parish of Liverpool was passed. A Select Vestry was to be elected to manage poor relief. It was to be 'deemed to be a Board of Guardians' with all the rights and duties of such a board. Twenty-one Vestrymen, subject to a property qualification of £50 rateable value, were to be elected at a parish meeting of the ratepayers, and, together with the rectors, churchwardens and overseers, they would form the management committee. This made twenty-nine in all. There was to be nothing 'to prevent any of the Persons filling the office of Guardians of the Poor from being elected'.

On 28 July 1842, a Special General Vestry was convened to elect the twenty-one members. Raymond Houghton, a leading Tory and churchwarden, proposed twenty-one names, and these were duly elected without a contest. Fourteen of them had been on the Board of Guardians. Some connection with the Poor Law Commission was retained, and the Liverpool statistics continued to be recorded in the annual reports and other documents. The chief consideration was the end of Charles Mott's influence, for in gaining exemption from the Poor Law Amendment Act, Liverpool had, in practice, freed the town from the inspectoral role of the Assistant Poor Law Commissioner.

Liverpool managed to journey through three phases of Poor Law history in less than a year and a half with hardly a tremor. The Reverend A. Campbell was chairman of this trio of ostensibly different committees. J. Mellor, E. Ford, J. Wilkinson, and W. Foster appeared on all three lists, and a score of others appeared in two. The two assistant overseers, E. Gray and J. Evans, sailed smoothly through these abrupt vacillations without apparent difficulty. The main difference in personnel was that the clergy, parish overseers, and churchwardens automatically enjoyed membership in both the old and the new Vestries. Men like Raymond Houghton had no need to present themselves to the electorate, and, after 1842, power was very firmly fixed in the Anglican and High Tory camp through this emphasis on parochial influence. Not that elections were familiar events; it is a strange fact that none of these three committees required any ballot at all, as the requisite number of candidates, and no more, was each time nominated as a bloc.

It is equally strange that the post-1835 reformed council showed little interest. Even though it was Tory-controlled at this time, the exercise of poor relief was then the nation's sole social service, and a more far-sighted council might have made some bid for influence in the new establishment. As for the Poor Law Commission it kept very quiet in its next annual report about this maverick development. As with some other local acts still governing poor relief, the commission had a certain amount of authority, as, significantly, in its 1843 report it was at pains to clarify. The commission was by law able to 'issue regulations . . . with respect to the administration of the poor', for a local act 'presupposes the general law on the subject'. There is no doubt that Liverpool was a special case, but there were probably other special cases. Liverpool's successful reappraisal of the new Poor Law underlines the damaging inflexibility with which the Poor Law reformers dogmatically reduced the country to an often harmful uniformity.

The Liverpool Vestry buckled down quickly to its job. As early as 1842 it was decided to reconstruct the workhouse on Brownlow Hill at a cost of £25,000 and to house 1,800 inmates. As always seems to be the pattern with public finance, the estimate was too low, and over subsequent years further loans amounting to nearly £12,000 were also raised. Loans had to be sanctioned by the Poor Law Commission—a vestigial remnant of its power in Liverpool. The commission was naturally eager to grant such permits for loans to be obtained from the Exchequer Loan Bill Commissioners. A weakness of the central body was that it could not oblige the local Board of Guardians to erect workhouses, and consequently it was always keen to support local initiative.

Liverpool Vestry soon built up a sizeable organisation. By 1849, it employed 187 officers, of whom 65 were full-time. Of these, 94 were teachers, full-time and part-time, in the Industrial Schools established by the Poor Law authorities 'to eradicate the baneful malady of hereditary pauperism', a preventive enterprise that was an instance rarely recalled of the public subsidy of education before 1870. But in A. Hume's *Condition of Liverpool*, published in 1858, the poor relief system was heavily criticised. The criticism pin-pointed a defect often to be discovered behind the 'union' façade in other areas, namely, the division of an area into districts which then became wellnigh independent so that the much advertised virtues of the larger entity were lost. Liverpool was 'treated every day as if it consisted of from forty to fifty district communities. . . . A district is regarded, with a few honourable exceptions, as if there were no human necessity beyond it or human sympathy within it'. Eleven of the thirty-six relieving districts had 54 per cent of the pauperism. It ranged hugely from a 42 per cent pauper population in St Stephen's district to 1 per cent in St George's district. Liverpool had always been proud of its system of investigation, but this essay threw doubts on the fairness and efficacy of the scheme, suggesting that responsibility, financial and otherwise, was disproportionately delegated.

Whatever the rights of this, the poor relief organisation was to be severely tested in the 1840s as the Irish immigration reached its peak. The Poor Law Commission's Annual Report of 1847 recorded 80,000 Irish in Liverpool alone. It was at this time that the Vestry switched from central to district relief to the anger of critics like Hume. The Vestry claimed, perhaps extravagantly, that this lowered the weekly cases relieved from 25,000 to between 4,000 and 10,000 weekly. But was this the Vestry getting less naïve or more miserly? Unless up to 21,000 paupers had each week pulled the wool over the Relieving Officer's eyes, it must have been the latter. District relief favoured the ratepayer rather than the pauper, and then, as Hume was later to point out, it treated both differentially according to district. It is said that in the first quarter of 1847, 144,000 Irish landed in Liverpool and only 16,000 of them moved on to the United States and Canada. Some, obviously, moved to other parts of Lancashire and the country at large. Bolton, for example, had 209 Irish relief cases in the opening quarter of 1846; it had 1,815 in the corresponding quarter of 1847, while even rural unions like Fylde and Garstang felt some impact from 'the influx of Irish'. Despite the 'unwearied exertions' of the Liverpool Vestry, mortality jumped alarmingly. In April 1846, 79 Irish paupers had died, and in April 1847 the figure rose disastrously to 586. Overcrowding, with all its attendant vices of unemployment, malnutrition, and disease, was the simple explanation. The town could not withstand nor absorb the wave of migration either socially or economically. It was reported that there were as many as forty-one lodgers in one four-roomed working-class house.

Dockland also provided by far the most noisome slums. Liverpool was not then especially suited to passenger traffic on the large scale, and even those merely travelling from Ireland, via Liverpool, on the Atlantic passage were subjected to days and often weeks of intolerable conditions. The bewildered Irish peasantry were fair game for the Liverpool 'land-sharks', whose depravity, Herman Melville wrote in 1849, was not equalled on any of the world's water-fronts. The 'runners', as the shipping touts were known, bamboozled the immigrants as they landed at Liverpool and rooked them for lodgings, supplies, and sea fare. They were organised into syndicates, the most ill-famed of which was called 'The Forty Thieves'. The consequences of this dreadful and fradulent trade pressed hard on Liverpool's poor relief.

There were two main results pertinent to Poor Law management. One was a predictable leap in expenditure. In the year ending March 1842 Liverpool's account for the maintenance of the poor was £35,000. In 1847 it was £67,000 and the following year it sprang to nearly £117,000; 1848 was one of the worst years for poor relief generally, when Manchester's bill was £125,000, and when Preston, Salford, and Warrington were three of many towns whose expenditure doubled. It was the year not only of peak immigration but of cholera, and not until the Great Cotton Famine was Lancashire to be so sorely tried. The other result was the breakdown of the Workhouse Test and the flouting of the principle that outdoor relief should be abolished. Pauperdom was harsh enough to make a nonsense of the idea that all paupers should retire to the workhouse. Grave economic dislocations, like the Irish Potato Famine or the American Civil War, had widespread manifestations in trade and employment. The 'less-eligibility' device for forcing workers on to the labour mart was valueless if no work was available. With tragic drama the Irish migrant demonstrated that the new Poor Law had mistaken symptom for cause. As late as 1855, when Liverpool life was on a more stable keel, 'out-paupers' still outnumbered 'in-paupers' by 45,000 to 28,000. Fifteen thousand cases of pauperism were being relieved each week, and this amounted to 5.6 per cent of the population.

It was the later 1860s before the Poor Law Vestry recovered from the fateful years of the Irish incursion. Nationally, the process of unionisation and, what was more important, the rationalisation of fiscal and audit supervision was completed. Liverpool, like many another area, settled down thereafter to a further sixty years of the Poor Law. Times were never quite so bad on the broad scale again, although the spectre of poverty rarely if ever departs from Merseyside. It was not until 1929 that the Poor Law was replaced by county and county borough supervision, by which time the cold regimen of the workhouse system had cut deep into the folk-memory of the British working-classes—it had been in 1877 that George R. Sims wrote for *The Sunday Referee* the much-parodied ballad 'It was Christmas Day in the Workhouse' in which he attacked the segregation of husband and wife practised in many workhouses.

A year or so beforehand William Rathbone, most famous of Liverpool's civic dignitaries of his epoch, criticised the workings of the Poor Law administration in a speech (later published in pamphlet form) in the House of Commons. He used Liverpool as his prime example and the speech serves as a fair summary to the busiest thirty or forty years in the town's Poor Law history. Rathbone went further than those who criticised discrimination within Poor Law areas. His main concern was with the injustice of some unions (more particularly those centred on large towns) being under weightier pressure than others. He argued sensibly for a uniform and national rate, with each citizen sharing the relief load equitably across the country. He demonstrated how the poor gravitated towards the large towns, as the Irish had done in the case of Liverpool. He told the anecdote of a Manxman who had four or five times visited the Liverpool Workhouse to be cured of a skin complaint; as the Liverpool Workhouse governor pithily commented, 'the Isle of Man had the benefit of his health and we had the expense of his sickness'. Given such pressure, the shortsighted policy of paying the officials badly resulted, and workhouse and relieving officials were too frequently 'half-educated and badly-trained men . . . who have failed in other departments of life'. In large towns there was also the 'impossibility of providing efficient supervision on the part of the Board of Guardians or Vestry' and the whole structure depended four-square on the paid officers. Area after area made 'the same costly blunders', said Rathbone, and Liverpool, by this time, was annually handling £190,000. He was later to object to the lack of identification of Poor Law and other administrative unities.

Rathbone's well-argued, informed and somewhat crushing indictment of Poor Law administration came on the eve of Gladstone's first ministry, usually regarded as the initiator of major collectivist legislation. It sufficiently post-dated the furore over the new Poor Law to escape any charge of jaundice, and his main points certainly held true of Lancashire's other sizeable towns. On the Poor Law reformers' own terms the system, although functioning effectively enough, was a partial failure. The elected boards could not sustain control, the 'expertise' was terribly inadequate, the costs had blown sky-high, central inspection was not always strenuous or incisive, and outdoor relief was more firmly entrenched than ever. Place against these administrative shortcomings the abhorrence felt for the new Poor Law, and one sees a structure getting the worst of both worlds. It was not fulfilling its own goal and it was unpopular.

The implications of Rathbone's critique were that social welfare should become completely a national responsibility. He was many years ahead of his time. In the meanwhile the Liverpool Poor Law authorities, having weathered the political and social storms of the forties, sailed stolidly on until 1929. It had always been an austere story; around 1840 the average cost of food per head in Kirkdale Gaol was 5s, while in the workhouse it was a mere 2s.

CHAPTER FIVE

The cholera and Doctor Duncan

Cholera was a Victorian near-equivalent of the medieval black death and replaced smallpox as the epidemic most to be feared in England. It attacked England most viciously on four occasions between 1830 and 1870, and Liverpool, a teeming overcrowded port, was to feel the brunt of the assault each time. In October of 1831 a case of Asiatic cholera was confirmed in Sunderland, and the disease spread quickly to Tyneside and Yorkshire. In April 1832 it arrived in Liverpool, believed to have come by way of Hull and York. In all it affected fourteen Lancashire towns, in particular Manchester, Salford, Warrington, Lancaster, and Wigan. The textile towns escaped relatively lightly. Liverpool had 4,912 official cases of cholera from the onset of the epidemic to the end of the year, an approximate average of 600 a month, and out of the 2,835 who died in Lancashire, 1,523 of them came from Liverpool, compared with Manchester's 1,267 cases and 706 deaths.

There followed the 1849 outbreak. There was a terrible slaughter resulting in 53,000 deaths from cholera in the United Kingdom, of which 8,000 were in Lancashire and no fewer than a tragic 5,308 in Liverpool, just 10 per cent of the national figure. Manchester lost this macabre competition with its great Lancastrian rival, for less than a thousand died in Manchester and the neighbouring textile towns again escaped lightly. No more dreadful sickness has ever so affected a town as hundreds died weekly through a long summer and into the early autumn. In one hot August week alone nearly six hundred people perished. More than one in a hundred died of cholera, with perhaps 15,000 to 20,000 actual cases in total. This time the disease, having made its way across the continent from India, had spread to Liverpool from Scotland. The last two epidemics, those of 1854 and 1866, were happily less destructive. Liverpool had 1,290 and 2,122 deaths respectively, out of Lancashire totals of 1,775 and 2,600. Again the numbers of dead formed the major proportion both of regional and national figures. In 1866 only some 400 cholera deaths in Lancashire were to be found outside the cramped confines of Liverpool, and the borough's dead contributed a ninth of the national total. *In toto* over 10,000 people in Liverpool died of cholera during the four outbreaks.

Sometimes the horror of a scourge such as cholera overwhelms the mind, but as part of a sad perspective, it must be recalled that other virulent diseases were active too. Typhus was another wretched fever which took a heavy toll of Liverpool life. In the last six months of 1837, 524 people died of typhus, and in the next two years nearly a thousand more succumbed. But 1847 was the peak year of the fever which, once known as 'gaol fever', changed its sorry soubriquet to 'Irish fever', just as it became known as 'famine fever' during the years of the cotton famine. In 1847 21,000 persons in Liverpool—one in fifteen of the population—died, and of these nearly a third died of typhus or one of its adjuncts. Although during the 1860s typhus added to the woes of the cotton towns like Preston, Accrington, or Blackburn, it still remained active on Merseyside.

Smallpox further added to the horrible story. In Liverpool, 880 persons died during a two and a half year epidemic from 1837 to 1839. Curiously, Exeter and Bath were the two other towns most grievously afflicted at this time. Lancashire as a whole was badly hit a year later, when over 3,000 died of smallpox, of whom 400 or so were Liverpolitans. During the full epidemic period more than 7,000 Lancastrians lost their lives. It makes an appalling narrative—four epidemics of cholera, one of smallpox and three of typhus, interlaced with sporadic cases of these and the general mournful run of respiratory, dysenteric and other diseases must all have cast a threatening shadow over Liverpool that is difficult to conceive today.

The reasons for these violent outbreaks of disease were obvious enough. The squalor and debilitation of Liverpool were earnestly and inexhaustibly recorded throughout much of the nineteenth century both in public reports and private commentaries. Four famous reports high-lighted the grave problems of Victorian public health and all of them turned to Liverpool for a telling contribution. The Select Committee on the Health of

Towns, reporting in 1840, included a contribution from John Riddall Wood: 'I was generally obliged to carry my handkerchief to my nose,' he confessed, as he toured the town's thoroughfares and streets, seeking out the filthy loci of fever and illness. W. H. Duncan, already well known locally, offered the first of his important national statements. He spoke of Liverpool's 2,400 closed courts, each with but one outlet and perhaps one privy to an entire court, in which 86,000 people lived, with 38,000 living in cellars. Spencer Court had had seventeen cases of fever during the preceding year and according to an Irish resident it entertained 'a smell bad enough to raise the roof of his skull'.

Duncan again weighed in with evidence for the 1842 Report on the *Sanitary Condition of the Labouring Population of Great Britain*, a document prepared by the Poor Law Commission, which was beginning to note the correlation between poverty and disease. 'I doubt whether there is a single court in Liverpool,' he averred, 'which communicates with the street by underground drain' and thus 'emanations from this pestilential surface' cause fever. In a year there had been sixty-three cases of fever in the twelve houses of Union Court, off Banastre Street and the 'whole court was inundated with fluid filth'. Riddal Wood (of the Manchester Statistical Society) also featured in the report with some gloomy statistics on overcrowding. In 1840, 5,597 members of the labouring classes had died in Liverpool, suggesting a frightening average life of only fifteen years for such persons.

In 1844 and 1845 the two reports of the Inquiry into the State of Large Towns and Populous Districts were published, and Duncan yet again produced shattering testimony of what he called the most unhealthy town in England. One-third of the working-class lived in courts and one-eighth in cellars. Only four of twenty miles of streets in working-class areas were sewered and Liverpool enjoyed the 'bad pre-eminence' of the worst population density in the provinces. An average of seven persons lived in each of the town's 32,000 houses. The lodging-houses were packed, often with thirty sleeping in a cellar, and other cellars were the sites for dames' schools, perhaps with forty young children jammed in a tiny basement. One in 400 of the population annually died of fever but, in the courts, the ratio rose acutely to one in thirty. Fifty-three per cent of the infants died before they were five. Lyon Playfair, a noted social commentator, contributed a survey of the

Liverpool situation in which he recorded the ludicrous ruling—
'a regulation peculiar to Liverpool'—that water-closets were not
to be connected with sewers. Samuel Holme, a local politician and
builder, gave evidence about the lack of 'proper necessaries'—as
he delectably described lavatories. 'I never hail anything', he said,
'with greater delight than I do a violent tempest, or a terrific
thunderstorm, accompanied by heavy rain, for these are the only
scavengers that thousands have to cleanse away any impurities
and the filth in which they live, or rather exist.'

These four documents certainly stimulated some action in the
public health field, but it was dilatory and hesitant action and
the problem accumulated substantially. The work of William
Farr, 'the father of vital statistics', of E. H. Greenbrow and Sir
John Simon demonstrates that medical needs had been little
relieved even forty years afterwards. Farr claimed that in Liverpool in 1870 the population was 66,000 to the square mile, a mean
proximity, incredibly, of only seven square yards for each person.
The death-rate was 39 in a 1,000 in 1870 and, compared with a
countrified area, Liverpool's statistics were decidedly gloomy.
The death-rate was nearly two and a half times higher and infant
mortality was three and a half times as bad as in healthy districts.
Liverpool had the worst death-rate in the country and one that
had worsened over much of the century; it had averaged 26 in
1,000 during the first three decades, but, between 1830 and 1890 it
rose to and was maintained at an average of 33 in 1,000. Anything
above 17 was, according to Farr, indicative of poor surround-
ings; while 'any rate above 30 implies sanitary conditions highly
destructive of human life'. In the 1840s the death-rate rose to 39.

Doctor Greenbrow, in *The Sanitary State of the People of England*, published in 1858, pointed to the huge infant mortality
rate in Lancashire, and especially Liverpool. A third of Liverpool's babies died during their first year. Both Greenbrow and
Farr were able easily to demonstrate the correlation of high death-
rates and overcrowding. Writing much nearer the end of the
century, Sir John Simon, a colleague of Greenbrow and the man
who became London's and then England's first medical officer of
health, looked back over forty years of strife. Lancashire, and
more particularly its two great conurbations, was in many ways
the unhealthiest region in the country. Apart from the ravages of
cholera, typhus and diarrhoea, the North West had the highest

Page 89 (*Above*) The second Liverpool Infirmary on Brownlow Hill, 1828; (*left*) Doctor Duncan

Page 90 (*Above*) The interior of a Victorian washhouse in Liverpool; (*right*) Christopher Bushell, first chairman of the Liverpool School Board

number of pulmonary afflictions, with a half as many again as the national norm dying from such complaints. Seven to ten out of every thousand died of lung and consumptive disorders, including the very heavy incidence of phthisis in textile areas. Scarlatina, whooping-cough, measles and smallpox were twice and thrice as rife in Liverpool and its surrounds as elsewhere. Around the 1860 era, only 57 per cent of Liverpool children were vaccinated, a figure much lower than the relatively high national figures. Acute non-infectious diseases were likewise prominent. Convulsive disorders resulted in the deaths of four and five out of every hundred children under the age of five. This was three times the rate for the country at large, and a seventh of the total deaths were caused by convulsions. Simon, with Chadwick, is one of the two foremost public health reformers of the century, and he was able to point out the cause succinctly: 'common sanitary defects', he claimed to be the major reason, caused by 'the foul air and foul water of undrained, unpaved, unscavenged, unwashed, unlighted, unventilated localities and housing'. In his campaign for massive public health programmes, Simon enunciated his famous aphorism that 'sanitary neglect is a mistaken parsimony'.

The man who led Liverpool's counter-attack against the emphatic assaults of ill health was William Henry Duncan. He was born in 1805, the year of Trafalgar, a victory which helped secure England's trading future and accentuate industrialism, and by the same token its grim aftermath. Cholera was the most devastating of the urban epidemics, and Duncan's career ran in curious parallel with its incidence in Liverpool. A graduate in medicine of Edinburgh University, then as now celebrated for its medical school, he started to practise in 1829 in Rodney Street, still locally known as 'Liverpool's Harley Street'. Like another famous Liverpolitan, Gladstone, born in Rodney Street in 1809, he had filial attachments to Scotland, and he was one of many doctors of Scottish extraction and training to practise in the north of England. A few months after he began work in 1829, he took on additional duties as a physician to the 'Liverpool Dispensaries', an institution catering for the destitute sick and supported in part by charity and in part by the parish. There were two agencies, the Liverpool North and the Liverpool South dispensaries, and it was at the former in Vauxhall Road that Duncan began to face the overwhelming issue of the deprived environment.

F

Duncan had scarcely settled to his twin life of fashionable consultant and physician to the poor when the first wave of cholera struck. Its horror can be gauged from the spectacular instance of a boat, anchored off Liverpool docks, with a complement of 349 of whom 83 died and most were suffering from cholera. The abrupt dysenteric and feverish symptoms of Asiatic cholera bowled over its victims with a vengeful, almost biblical, swiftness. Duncan's dispensary work immediately faced him boldly with an epidemic of frightening proportions, but, like all the other public health reformers of the epoch, he attempted to measure the correlations of disease to environment and propagate the point accordingly. Writing in 1833 in the *Liverpool Medical Gazette*, he analysed the 216 cases (56 deaths) he attended personally. Whereas there were 97 cases each in cellars and courts, there were only 26 living in houses. Only a seventh of these died, while a quarter in cellars, courts, and lodging-houses succumbed. He warned against the temptations of Victorian statistics by his allegation that the South Dispensary showed 800, not the more accurate 300, cases of cholera, in an attempt to impress on people that the South Dispensary was every bit as fine as Duncan's northern outpost in Vauxhall Road. Emergency epidemic sheds had to be opened at Lime Street and Toxteth Park.

The hastily established Liverpool Board of Health attempted to meet an overwhelmingly difficult situation with instructions published in the press. The *Liverpool Mercury* printed the board's wishes that 'a speedy separation of the patient from the healthy, by removing him to the hospital, is most earnestly advised'. They strongly urged that 'in no cases are any apprehensions to be entertained of anatomical examinations after death'. This was an attempt to repair the sad breakdown of trust between doctors and patients which had occurred both in Liverpool and Manchester. 'Among great numbers of the lower classes in this town', said the *Mercury*, 'the idea is prevalent that the cholera is a mere invention of the medical men to fill their own pockets.' Many panic-stricken folk thought that their hospitalised friends and relatives were, as the *Mercury* described it, 'the victims of experiments while living and subjects for the dissecting knife when dead'. It is likely that fire lay under the ugly smoke of rumour and that not all the medicos were guiltless of illicit dissection, for this was the prime era of the body-snatcher. No commentator has noticed that the cholera epidemic came immediately after the hideous affair of Burke and Hare, nor has it been observed that Burke was executed in Edinburgh in the same year that Duncan graduated there. His studies and Burke's body-raising coincided, and Duncan was bound at some stage to have been a student under Dr Knox for whom Burke and Hare arranged their macabre supply. Whether the rumours were true or false, the crowds assembled to prevent the removal of patients and surgeons were mobbed when officiating over transfers to hospitals.

'The very disgraceful outrages to which the medical gentlemen of Liverpool have been subjected', led the doctors, so the *Liverpool Mercury* reported, to threaten 'to leave the people to their fate.' Merseyside has had its fair share of strikes, but this would have been one of the oddest. As it was, T. H. Bickerton, author of *A Medical History of Liverpool* and a constant apologist for the medical profession, felt able to conclude that the doctors 'lived down the evil reputation earned in the newspaper controversy by their devoted and usually gratuitous service'. As well as sharp exchanges in the press over the conduct of doctors, there were wildly varying contests over the efficacy of treatments. W. W. Squires, who wrote a revealing article in 1833 for the *Liverpool Medical Gazette* entitled 'Cholera Epidemica as it appeared in Liverpool', was in charge of the cholera hospitals, and he underlined the discussions as to whether mercury, opium, stimulants, or purgatives were most efficacious. Tobacco enemas were another grisly remedy widely used. Squires was most hard on the very popular use of saline injections, the salt being presumed to replace the racking, wasting nature of the disease. For his part, he felt that 'depressing passions' and 'terror' were often the causes of cholera. It might be wondered whether the miseries of the cures were another reason for the people's reluctance to enter hospital.

Squires, too, was rightly annoyed by the plentiful presence of quacks and by the eager and incredulous snatching up of their useless branded cures. Naturally he put his faith in hospitalisation. In one refuge house of 150 patients only 4 died; his figures are, however, a little doubtful. He claimed that Duncan treated 806 cases, whereas Duncan admitted to no more than 300. Squires complained that families left it much too late to allow sick relations to enter hospitals, but in a moment of valuable revelation he confesses that he had to stop dissecting. What he called 'popular excitements' led to the practice being banned.

Duncan had had the good fortune to attend Edinburgh University medical school, the only British university to have copied the continental model of having a chair in medical jurisprudence. Here he must have learned of the Germanic theory, normally associated with Professor Johann Peter Frank, of a 'medical police', what now we would call a public health authority. The cholera epidemic drove home the practical lesson that health depends on a community responsibility, and he thereafter never tired in his efforts to raise the standards of public as well as private health. It was from this point that he began his long list of contributions in favour of the public health reform movement. Writing in the *Liverpool Medical Gazette* immediately after the epidemic, he warned that 'fever prevails at all times to a greater or lesser extent among the poor of Liverpool and must continue to prevail so long as their inhabitations are so systematically contrived how best to accumulate filth and exclude the air of heaven'. Duncan became prominent in the Liverpool branch of the Health of Towns Association, he frequently wrote in its journal, the *Health of Towns Advocate*, he lectured in medical jurisprudence in the Liverpool medical school, he became a consultant to the Liverpool infirmary, he was a member of the Liverpool Athenaeum, and he was a president of the Liverpool Medical Institutes.

He was soon well known nationally as a public health propagandist. Like many of the leading and progressive doctors of the time, Duncan believed in the 'miasmic' theory of disease induction. The idea was that 'poisonous exhalations' rose in the form of gases from garbage, sewage, and filth to create a 'miasma' or atmosphere which carried diseases. Overcrowding in unsanitary conditions was at the root of the trouble, and Duncan and the 'environmentalists' or 'clean party' were anxious to produce a hygienic context from which little or no 'poisonous exhalations' could arise. The germ theory and most of the work of Koch and Snow was in the future, and Duncan, in effect, saw the right cause of disease for the wrong reasons. Quarantining and the removal of patients from the 'miasma' meant that personal contacts were reduced and this was especially important with a sickness like cholera which was later shown to be transferred via excrement. Similarly the large-scale whitewashing, which Duncan was to promote on the grounds that it decontaminated the 'miasma', had some antiseptic function. Again, the constipative drugs that were widely used acted as some brake on the likelihood of infection. These were prescribed officially in the General Board of Health's Report on Cholera in 1849: 20 grains of opiate confection mixed with 2 tablespoons of peppermint-water, or with a little weak brandy and water repeated every three or four hours, or oftener, if the attack is severe, until the looseness of the bowels is stopped; or an ounce of chalk mixture, with 10 or 15 grains of the aromatic confection and from 5 to 10 drops of laudanum, repeated in the same manner . . .'.

Prior to his contributions to the famous national reports of the forties, Duncan had secured his local reputation with solid evidence to the 1833 Inquiry into the Corporation of Liverpool and the 1835 Inquiry into the State of the Irish Poor. He forcefully put the points that there were thousands of cellar-dwellers and court-dwellers in Liverpool, and that the worst of these cellars and courts contained the Irish poor, amounting to a third of the town's poor. Duncan claimed that the vast proportion who died in the recent cholera epidemic had been Irish and that several hundreds of deaths more had not been notified. His judgement on the Irish was harsh, for they seemed to him 'to be as contented amidst dirt and filth and close foul air as in clean and airy situations'. Sometimes he found himself in contention. A local surgeon, John P. Halton, accused him of bringing notoriety to the 'good old town', and Duncan, always ready for a verbal scrap, published a scathing pamphlet in reply, supporting his calculation that the average age of death in Liverpool was nineteen.

Eventually the propaganda and exposures told. The Liverpool Sanitary Act of 1846 was passed and it was the most comprehensive and far-reaching health legislation so far to be introduced. It included powers to appoint a Medical Officer of Health, and a Special Committee recommended Duncan to the post, recognising his part 'in directing popular attention to the question of sanitary improvement'. A move to make this a full-time appointment at £700 per annum was defeated in council by twenty-five votes to eight, and Duncan was appointed to a part-time post at £500. Just as Liverpool was the first town to receive a thorough-going public health statute, it was the first to appoint a permanent Medical Officer of Health. For these things Liverpool deserves just credit, but it must be remembered that Liverpool needed them more than most, being, in Duncan's own words, 'the unhealthiest town in England'.

No sooner was Duncan and the new Health Committee appointed than the typhus fever rampaged through the poorer areas, in particular the Vauxhall and Scotland wards, in the wake of the 1847 increase in Irish immigration. Seven-eighths of the victims were Irish, the majority of them newly arrived. Diarrhoea, dysentery, measles, and smallpox were also taking a grim toll. In Duncan's first year as MOH over 21,000 people—one in fifteen of the population—died. One-third, that is 470, of the inhabitants of Lace Street died. The council resolved to make Duncan's a full-time appointment with a salary of £750, despite the opposition of the *Liverpool Mercury*, of Councillor Cooper (who thought the £750 should be used for whitewashing the town) and of Councillor Evans (who thought Duncan's work need not be done by a medical man). The year 1848 was better, although scarlatina reached epidemic proportions and carried off 1,500 victims. But in December 1848, with Duncan only just settled in full-time office, the second and most desolating Asiatic cholera epidemic began.

The unfriendly *Mercury* was prepared to accuse Duncan of murder for his refusal to acknowledge the diagnoses and magical pills of a certain Doctor Hawthorne, one of several charlatans claiming an infallible cure for cholera. Duncan, however, was much too busy to be concerned with such wild accusations, having embarked on a massive operation of house-to-house visitation and lime-washing in an effort to stem the onslaught. In the week ending 18 August 1849 no fewer than 572 deaths were notified, and Duncan was horrified to find mass burials becoming habitual, with as many as a hundred corpses flung into a single open pit. A Medical Relief Committee was established and immediately began a lengthy wrangle with Duncan on the rights and wrongs of each other's actions. While they argued the epidemic continued, and, apart from the 5,000 and more who died officially of cholera, there were probably hundreds more whose cause of death was wrongly interpreted as diarrhoea or dysentery.

None the less, the implementation of the Sanitary Act slowly began to make good the years of sanitary neglect. Duncan and his fellow officers worked staunchly to provide a hygienic environment, toiling to provide cleansing water and sewerage services, to inspect lodging-houses and slaughterhouses and cemeteries and to have cesspools, smoke and other pollutions abated. The Irish influx and the consequent ravages of disease complicated matters, but some progress was made. The relatively light incidence of the 1854 cholera epidemic was, in part, the result of such advances.

A central feature of the Health Committee's work was the controversial clearance of the cellars. Some had been cleared and filled in under an Act of 1842, but many had been illegally re-entered by the incoming Irish. The 1846 Act gave increased powers for cellar clearance and Duncan and his colleages went about their task with determined vigour. By 1851 probably 10,000 'illegal street cellars' had been dealt with, most of them in 1847 and 1848. Possibly 30,000 people were evicted, and although the process was later limited to one hundred a month, in the early days thousands found themselves on the streets at once. Precious few houses were being built at that time at rentals even remotely realistic for the Irish paupers, and fever was rife about the town. In such unprepossessing circumstances, it must be confessed that whatever the general benefit to the community, the individual suffering consequent on wholesale cellar clearance was considerable. It had the effect of placing an even more enormous strain on the courts and lodging-houses, simply because eviction was organised without regard for alternative accommodation. In the blunt words of Thomas Burke, author of *A Catholic History of Liverpool*, Duncan and his friends, 'blundered badly'. A further point was that many of the cellar-dwellers were illiterate and could not read their eviction notices, a civic illiteracy that was becoming increasingly embarrassing in an evermore complex society and was to become an argument in favour of public education.

The cholera epidemic of 1854 came and went, reaching only a fifth of the intensity of its predecessor. The public quarrel between Duncan and the Medical Relief Committee continued, however, unabashed and undiminished. In 1858 an outbreak of scarlatina resulted in the death of over 1,100 children, while another 520 children died of measles that same year. Apart from disease, neglect was a constant cause of child death. In 1858, 79 dead infants were 'overlain by their mothers'. Infant mortality continued to be agonisingly high, and of 12,900 deaths in 1861, 6,500 were children under five. A hundred children died from diphtheria and 780 children died of whooping-cough, with tuberculosis another heavy cause of death, usually accounting for 2,000 or so each year. Put another way, the dramatic incursions of cholera tended sometimes to lead to a neglect of less spectacular but more sustained diseases. It would seem that, for the Liverpool poor, there were a dozen deaths awaiting round every corner. Gradually, however, the death-rate dropped a little as medical and sanitary amenities improved.

Duncan was combatively proud of these slight improvements. Although the first to recognise how much remained to be done, he attacked his critics with a most unmedical-like venom. He was deserving of some success, for he was a highly competent and conscientious man who, throughout his public career, had never received an increase in salary, nor ever had any permanent staff. His weekly reports to the Health Committee and all his other copious correspondence and reportage were written in his own hand. He literally fought the disease of a great town single-handed. His diligent, strenuous and selfless service lasted sixteen years, and by good fortune he never contracted any of the diseases he daily faced with such courage and resource, yet he never spared his own health in the struggle to protect that of his fellow-citizens. Worn down by the uneven contest, he died after a lingering illness in 1863 among his relations in Elgin, Scotland. He was fifty-seven, and he was still in the service of the corporation.

The *British Medical Journal* said that to his writings and work might 'be mainly traced the origin of the sanitary movement which has taken place in the country'. The *Liverpool Daily Post*, whilst paying him a tribute, recommended that the post could now revert to a part-time appointment. The council rightly thought otherwise. Dr W. S. Trench was Duncan's full-time successor. There was no going back, and once more almost on cue, the 1866 cholera epidemic paid its painful visit and over 2,000 Liverpolitans perished.

Today perhaps ten in every thousand die in Liverpool each year. Where Duncan began his awesome task, it was touching forty. Disease is not destroyed. Cholera struck again mildly in 1893, and as late as 1901 the occasional case of smallpox and plague was to be discovered in the port of Liverpool. Again, the winter of 1889–90 was to see the first of the influenza epidemics in

England, although by the last quarter of the century the wildfire epidemics were left far behind. Gradually Liverpool developed a public health service which was to win for itself an international reputation. Cholera drove home the lessons of public health with a disturbing cogency, and in Liverpool Duncan was the first to learn and apply the lessons effectively. As the first permanent Medical Officer of Health to be appointed in Great Britain, many of the public health developments not only of the city but of the country are traceable to his stance and efforts.

CHAPTER SIX

The struggle for water and drains

Because of its exaggeratedly unhealthy and filthy state, Victorian Liverpool illustrated in heavy tones the public health problem of urban England. The present-day simplicity of easily turned taps and quickly flushed lavatories is very much taken for granted, but the establishment of the sanitary norm enjoyed now is not even a hundred years old, and its completion is barely completed. The fight to construct the public format for community health was slow and bitter, with Liverpool not least in the forefront because of its abnormally sorry condition. Hygiene, public or private, is rarely a pleasurable topic, and is often as dull as it is noisome. Few school history textbooks refer in detail to the construction of water and sewage works, preferring to regale their readers with tales of derring-do and do-goodery. This had been a Victorian difficulty. Reports on sanitation were sometimes censored or withdrawn from public view on the grounds of obscenity, and there were many who refused to believe these sanitary atrocity stories. Yet it is arguable that urban civilisation rests on its capacity to cleanse itself by the provision of water and drainage. Liverpool now enjoys some international repute for its public health services, which include, at base, the securing each day of up to 30 million gallons of water and the removing of 750 tons of sewage, as well as a countless bulk of other waste and effluent.

The issue of urban hygiene arose urgently with the demographic explosion of the late eighteenth and early nineteenth centuries, particularly in so far as this was associated with overcrowding in the towns. At the accession of Queen Victoria the population of Liverpool had more than doubled since the beginning of the century. At a conservative estimate of 8 gallons per person per day (present standards allow between 30 and 40 gallons) this inferred that Liverpool required 600 million gallons of water each year. It also meant that there was 120,000 tons of sewage to be disposed of, together with all the domestic and mercantile refuse of a crowded port. In that the population had increased so briskly it was a problem that presented itself abruptly to an age as yet unversed in many of the complexities of civil engineering. The problem was not just cholera and the attendant diseases, although these certainly alarmed the citizenry and occasioned much of the progress; it was, in addition, the sheer discomfort and intolerable inconvenience of constantly living in a muckheap. This was bad for health, bad for trade, bad for social intercourse. The pragmatic evidence of the senses, as well as the realisation that fever cared not for social gradations, forced the town's middle-class to act.

Water was the key. Victorian sanitary enthusiasts excited themselves over the so-called 'arterial-venous' system, with the veins pumping in the water from the countryside in order to swill the sewerage from the towns into active service as fertiliser in the rural areas. It was naively hoped that this exercise in perpetual motion would be self-supporting. Liverpool certainly had a long way to go before such a pastoral idyll could even be imagined. Water was provided mainly by two companies, the Bootle Company and the Liverpool and Harrington Company, and in 1845 the Liverpool Guardian Society for the Protection of Trade, significantly enough, requested an inquiry into the business of water supply. It was, said the Society, 'not only miserably inadequate but the most expensive in the country', and they quoted the Bootle and Liverpool Companies' shares which stood respectively at three times and six times their face value. Five thousand people signed the memorial of complaint and a Special Committee of the Highways Board was mounted to prepare a report 'on the alleged dearness and insufficiency of water in Liverpool'.

The Highways Board may seem a strange choice, but then the whole field was beset by oddity. Apart from the two private companies the Commissioners for Paving and Sewers controlled what paving and sewerage existed, whereas the Health Committee, newly formed in 1842, supervised the drainage of Liverpool's many courts. The Highways Board, another set of local statutary commissioners, watered the streets, but the Corporation by means of—even more strangely—its Watch Committee, was responsible for cleaning them. Further, the Council ran the fire brigade but the Commission controlled the water available for fire-fighting. The old Improvement Commission existed side by side as yet with the Town Council and it was to the Highways Board, which at least had some connection with watering, that the trading fraternity turned.

There had been no less than ten improvement Acts passed on behalf of Liverpool since 1786, but there was little to show for them. The Liverpool Company had 5 wells around the town and the Bootle Company had 11 boreholes and 3 sandstone reservoirs. For its part, the old corporation had dabbled with a 'Town Springs Company' as early as 1799, and although a couple of pumping stations had been erected, the move had been an abortive one. The two rival companies claimed to serve so many houses apiece that the joint total came to more than the actual number of houses in the borough. It was an embittered rivalry, with company workers occasionally indulging in fisticuffs as they fought over the digging up of a street and the laying of a pipe, rather like cattle ranchers caught up in contesting land claims in the Wild West. For all their bravado and feuding, the results were puny. The supply was intermittent and impure. Having water on tap possibly meant a supply for fifteen minutes at eleven o'clock at night twice a week. A court of a dozen or twenty hovels would be lucky to have one tap, while ten courts, ostensibly on tap, had had no water for three years. To take specific examples, the 52 inhabitants of Banastre Street had but one tap among them, and Chartres Street with 800 people in its 100 or so houses, had 24 taps. Each tap operated for a little over an hour three times a week, sometimes at six in the morning. Moreover, a householder might pay up to £10 a year for this sporadic privilege, a massive account even by today's rating.

The poorer people were known to queue for two or three hours for water, perhaps rising at four o'clock in the morning to make sure of a quota. Things were no better in the outlying districts. Villages like Woolton relied on springs and the 'dumb well', mere store quarries in which rainwater collected. The theft of water was common, and was quoted in governmental reports as a normal means by which the poor obtained water. A chief reason why hernia figured high in Victorian morbidity lists was that water had to be carried long distances by hand. Liverpool was just beginning its pioneering work with baths and wash-houses, and the Frederick Street bathhouse opened in 1842, was the first of its kind in the country. These were dependent on the goodwill of men like William Rathbone and on the labours of such as the legendary, if overrated, Catherine Wilkinson. They were evidence of the active disquiet of some citizens about the town's health affairs. Samuel Holme, a leading Liverpool politician with a sincere commitment to its hygiene problems and an acquaintance and discipline of Edwin Chadwick, had in 1843 published an attack, *Want of Water*, on the situation, which led to a reply entitled *Water: A Pamphlet by Harwood Banner*. Banner was a director of the Liverpool and Harrington Company and Holmes and he sustained a verbal battle which helped precipitate the 1845 inquiry and continued thereafter. It was taken up by the *Liverpool Mercury*. Banner accused Holme in its columns of 'rambling generalities and ebullitions of personal feelings towards myself', but the *Mercury* came out in full support of the water reformers, attacking what it described as 'the grasping avarice and tyrannical oppression' of the companies.

With this sort of disturbing testimony and in this kind of electric atmosphere, the findings of the Special Committee were predictable: 'the inhabitants ought not to be dependent upon mere trading companies for a supply of that most necessary article of life, but that the supply should be in the hands of a public body'. The time was ripe for this semi-socialist sentiment, for Liverpool was on the eve of its vital Sanitary Act of 1846. This enabled the Council to take over the powers of most other related bodies, like the Highways Board, and sophisticate and extend those powers. The Green Lane Wells, for instance, used by the Highways Board for street cleaning, were immediately taken on by the Council and its much-strengthened Health Committee.

In 1847 the Council, thus empowered, turned its attentions wholeheartedly to the question of water supply. With new plans laid for sanitation, fire protection and street cleaning as well as domestic and commercial supply, an estimated 8 million gallons was required daily. The approximation of individual usage each day began to rise above 10 and approach 20 gallons, each lavatory flushing, it should be recalled, needing 2 or more gallons. With some expedition, the Council obtained a statute, the Liverpool Corporation Waterworks Act, by which it was able to buy out the two companies. The compensation amounted to £537,000, a very substantial sum when the insufficiency and greediness that had characterised these enterprises is considered. Having overcome, at that sacrificial price, the formidable opposition of the private companies, the corporation had now to resolve the knotty question of expansion.

There then ensued one of the most spectacular rows in the annals of Liverpool municipal government. Two widely varying schemes were proposed. One planned a gigantic artificial undertaking in the vicinity of Rivington Pike, near Chorley, which would draw on the Rivers Douglas and Riddlesworth and eventually conserve up to 3,000 million gallons. The other was less ambitious and was in part a hangover from the old water companies in pattern and advocacy. This proposed a more intense deployment of the existing sandstone springs around Liverpool, coupled with the utilisation of Lake Bala in North Wales as a natural reservoir. In practice, the former was a major and the latter a minor modification and much of the division was really between those who approached the question positively and those who approached it negatively. A fiery debate, in press, in private lobby, and on public platform raged, and it was soon obvious that the argument ranged round the Rivington Pike scheme and whether the massive outlay involved was either viable or desirable. So much was this true that the contestants were dubbed the Pikists and anti-Pikists.

The Rivington Pike scheme had been devised in 1846–7 by three water engineers, one of whom was Thomas Hawsley, perhaps the most noted water expert of this or any other era. They had assiduously inspected the range of possibilities and conceived of this mammoth proposal. Those who advanced the view that local sources should be tapped were chiefly concerned with cost, and ammunition was all too readily at hand. The initial estimate in 1847 was £200,000, but by 1850 it was £450,000 and the ultimate cost was to be £1,346,000, to say nothing of the £537,000 already paid in purchase of the two water companies. As so often happens with civic designs, over-enthusiasm led to underpricing, and W. Bennett and J. R. Jeffery were able, month by month, to demonstrate the extravagance of the proposition. In leading the anti-Pikist revolt, they also seized on the accepted fact that other Lancashire towns were obviously going to benefit from the work and then from the water supply. Whereas the Pikists viewed this

with charitable detachment, their opponents saw it as an unnecessary burden.

In the beginning the Pikists obtained a council majority and in
this as throughout the tortuous negotiations, they owed much to
their leader, George Holt. Parliamentary assent was obtained, and
then in 1850 there was a reversal of the political situation, and the
anti-Pikists in the council chamber discovered themselves to be
in the ascendant. Their joy was short-lived. They realised that
George Holt was as acute and watchful in execution as he had
been patient and tactful in legislation. The contracts for the construction of Rivington Pike waterworks had been signed and
sealed and it was legally difficult for the corporation to renegue.
However, an attempt was made and a court of inquiry mustered.
The chief inspector was no less than Robert Stephenson, the railway engineer who also interested himself in civil engineering. On
28 March 1850 he reported favourably on the Rivington Pike
scheme and the council sensibly abided by his arbitration. It was
a necessary decision, not just a wise one. The determination to
stand by local and natural resources was understandable but
short-sighted, for the problem was, of course, not a stationary one.
While the wrangling had continued, thousands more had by birth
or immigration joined Liverpool's population, each one a bid for
10 or 15 gallons of water a day.

Work was begun in 1852. Typically of Victorian civil engineering, a science still in its infancy, there were vacillations and snags
and troubles of all kinds, and time passed and costs soared. No
fewer than six amending Acts in the 1850s contained sections
devoted to the Rivington scheme, the chief one of them being
the 1856 statute which allowed for the purchase of Chorley waterworks on the Rivington site and the consequent intersection of
Chorley and Liverpool water supplies, anathema to the Bennett-
Jeffery group. Nevertheless, by 1857 the Rivington waterworks
were in full swing. There were five reservoirs in all, covering 500
acres, and the predicted 3,000 million gallons were available. A
constant water supply was now available to Liverpool and other
districts, as yet outside the municipal borders, were keen to take
advantages of this enormously rich reserve. There were still
technical difficulties, all of which the anti-Pikists, fighting a vain
and enfeebled rearguard action, were apt to broadcast. It was not
until 1860 that the public company felt able to furnish water for

baths and water-closets without a fairly heavy extra charge. Until the filter beds matured, the water suffered from a sickly yellowy appearance, a certain winner for the anti-Pikist faction and the pure water traditionalists. There was also a disturbing amount of seepage through defective piping, and another two amending statutes, in 1862 and 1866, were necessary to repair this heavy wastage. In effect, Liverpool has benefited from a full-run, constant, cheap and publicly controlled water supply for just over a century. Given the manifold difficulties, the enterprise was a decidedly meritorious one and Liverpool was one of the first of the large towns to tackle the problem with energy and dispatch. Warrington, for instance, did not form a municipal company until 1891. On this sturdy foundation Liverpool looked forward to the increasing pressures on its water supply with confidence and, in the present century, the city of Liverpool pursued in depth one tenet of anti-Pikist policy, in that it developed large tracts of mid-Wales for water provision.

Concurrently, there was the drainage and sewage issue. Water-driven sewerage was, of course, impossible without ceaseless, high velocity water. Contrarily, water supply was a menace if no drainage existed to run off the effluent and surplus. And Liverpool drainage was in a parlous condition. In 1732 'a proper person was employed to take away dirt from the streets' and ten years later he was joined by another, doubtless equally 'proper', along with a cart and bell. There had been little advance on this by 1840 by way of street cleaning, and only a few of the major highways were crudely sewered. Street cleaning sometimes did more harm than good. A letter in the *Liverpool Mercury* in 1840, signed by 'Cymro', pointed out that the throwing of sand and gravel over the dirt and excrement in the streets made for a peculiarly vile mud which, apart from its aesthetic limitations, positively hindered trade. Here again the commercial interest told. The wheels of commerce were hampered by filthy roadways which repulsed clients and blocked transport. Just as the merchants (many of whom had private domestic provision) were concerned about water because an abundant supply relieved their anxieties over warehouse and shop fires, there was also a strong economic reason for scavenging the streets.

The sewers that did exist were the large, brick or wooden square-shaped ones, big enough to allow the entry of an intrepid

Page 107 Chatsworth Primary School, one of Liverpool's first Board Schools, still active today

workman to clean them, big and slow enough also to be useless
for the transportation of solids. This is probably the explanation of
that strange Liverpool regulation which at one time forebade
water-closets to be linked with the sewers. This paradox has long
puzzled commentators, one or two of whom have seen in this
ruling the obtuse workings of the bureaucratic mind. However,
it was no use having water-closets making deposits in sewers
which could not carry them; alternately, imagination fails at the
concept of a wc with no such outlet.

The Highway Board had in fact laid fifty miles of sewers between 1830 and 1856 in the main thoroughfares, but these generally served only as flood-drains. A small scavenging force was
unequal to the strain of competing with Liverpool's daily harvest
of refuse and ordure, and, as elsewhere, the town was forced to
turn to contractors. Refuse depots and middens were located at
strategic points for the subcontractors to cart the deposit away
for sale to farmers. This programme had several shortcomings.
There was no correlation between what was strategic for the
contractor and for the citizen. The 'rich town guano' was prefer-
ably removed from the periphery of the town where the journey
was shorter and this tended to leave vast 'dung-mountains', as they
were called in Manchester, at less accessible spots. These literally
grew to thousands of tons in volume. Moreover, the demand for
manure was seasonal; it was heaviest in winter and early spring,
and lightest in summer and autumn during harvesting, when unluckily the weather was hottest—to the detriment both of health
and sensibility. In addition, the authorities found it necessary to
employ their meagre scavenging corps in clearing up after the
contractors had supposedly finished their assignment. It was a
sorry business.

Over and over, empirical assessment and statistical evidence
demonstrated the correlation of ill health and unsanitary sur-
roundings. Water supply was the given answer, and in its service
Edwin Chadwick and his cronies preached the terracotta pipe
dogma. This was the small, egg-shaped pipe able to transmit
water at high velocity and (despite some grievous accidents of
breakage and backwash) which was soon seen to be indispensable
for a wide-scale sanitary operation. People could scarely believe
that such tiny drains could replace the old man-sized ducts, partly
because they were convinced they could not be cleaned—the

answer was, of course, that they were self-cleansing. Concurrent, then, with the agitation for a municipalised waterworks was the campaign for a comprehensive sanitary service. The 1846 Sanitary Act, usually regarded as the nation's pioneer overall public health statute, gave wholesale powers to the Council, despite the opposition of the Highways Board and other bodies and commissions previously created by Improvement Acts. It enabled the Council to levy rates for paving, sewerage and general sanitation, and to appoint officers such as a Borough Engineer and an Inspector of Nuisance as well as a Medical Officer of Health. It gave imperative authority to the Health Committee, established with but sparse powers four years before, and the Health Committee became, in effect, England's first all-purpose local sanitary authority.

John Newlands was appointed first Borough Engineer and his function was to do for sanitation what Duncan had done for social and preventative medicine. In 1858 he read a paper, subsequently published, to the public health section of the National Association for the Promotion of Social Science. It was entitled *Liverpool Past and Present in relation to Sanitary Operations* and it provides an excellent primer on the opening phase of sanitary reform as it moved in partnership with improved water supply. He described the problem as he had found it. Previous legislation had failed owing to the sacrosanct nature of property rights: 'inferior considerations', he said, 'triumphed over the public good.' He took Albert Street as a microcosm of the whole; it was 290 yards long by 5 yards wide, its total area of street, courts, and buildings was nearly 8,000 square yards and 2,000 persons dwelt in the 200 houses there. This was 9 to a dwelling 4 square yards apiece and with no outlet for refuse or sewage. He reminded his audience that all the few sewers did was to drain off surface water and that house drains, let alone domestic sewers, could not be connected 'and thus for purposes of housing, they were a mockery'. By 1842 a biggish jump in scavengers, to a few dozen in number, had been managed, but the town was entirely 'boulder-stone paved', which made for severe difficulties. He recalled that there were 45,000 living in cellars and these could do no other except stack their rubbish and ordure in the street. There had been, he summarised, 'no steady endeavour to carry on sanitary operations on sound principles as preventive measures; in place we see spasmodic efforts during periods of alarm'.

The struggle for water and drains

Newlands himself was not averse to seizing on 'periods of alarm', and although he failed to mention this he could claim it as legitimate when, for instance, his far-reaching and massive plan of 1848 was accepted in the shadow of a cholera outbreak. Even then it required lengthy Council deliberations before his programme of a comprehensive borough system was ratified. This programme was incorporated in Newlands' Borough Engineer's Report to the corporation. In the report he suggested a scheme of underground water-driven drainage 'to fertilise the surrounding land'. It combined the small earthenware feeder pipes with huge outlet courses at the periphery of the system. He also requested 164 men and 18 sweeping machines (probably of the type invented by Whitworth, the Manchester engineer whose other blessings on mankind included work on the hydraulic beer-handle and water-closet). These were required immediately at a cost of £15,000, with water at a further cost of £3,000. Newlands reckoned that each man could on this basis keep 7,500 yards of streetway cleansed over a year. The rate needed would be a 9d one, 4d more than the outdated and ineffective system, which Newlands felt was reasonable enough. J. A. Tinne, chairman of the Health Committee, and men of social conscience such as William Rathbone, shepherded the report through, although the water controversy was raging and the landlords, led by the Earl of Sefton, were antagonistic. Even so, the objections were such that the Sanitary Amendment Act of 1854 was needed to elaborate and aid procedure and to permit the Medical Officer to certify houses for water-closet conversion if a health hazard existed.

Ten years later John Newlands looked proudly back on his endeavours and rehearsed them for the National Association for the Promotion of Social Science. Productivity had been immense. Bath-house users had risen from 12,000 to 273,000 and wash-house users from 10,000 to 64,000, and 2,000 streets, an increase of 500 and a gross length of 200 miles, were now cleaned regularly. There had been 53 miles of sewers in 1847. Another 80 miles of sewers had been added in the decade, together with 66 miles of main drains feeding a vast 6-mile outlet 6ft by 4ft in cross-section. At 17s per yard the whole system had cost the rate-payer a little over £215,000. Not least of Newlands' successes was that this was less than half the price of the 53 miles constructed prior to 1847. Newlands, of course, was also associated with the controversial cellar evictions, which he defended stoutly and maintained that 'healthy habitations were simultaneously provided'.

One must take this assertion with a pinch of salt, but, all in all, it was a colossal achievement, and at the time of the Borough Engineer's address the whole system was just receiving the full force of the new Rivington Pike enterprise. John Newlands had not left the detail within his broad framework to chance. Water-hydrants had multiplied, pits had been filled, public conveniences had been erected, smoke and other nuisances and pollutions had been partially abated, ashpit emptying had been controlled and intramural burial—one of the most horrifying of Victorian scandals throughout the land—had been regulated. Scavengers now numbered well over three hundred and, as paving improved, the expenditure dropped. It was reduced from £14,000 in 1847 to £10,000 in 1857, although a quarter more streets were being cleaned. A total of 5,000 new gullies had been provided and almost 4,000 renovated to shift surface water, while 257 new streets, a matter of 40,000 yards, had been paved and adopted as highways by the corporation. Most houses now had water and many had baths and lavatories, and 11,000 new houses, well-ventilated and equipped, had been built under the planning regulations. Newlands argued that as early as 1850 300 lives were saved by improved sanitation and that in 1857 the figure was 3,000.

It was an impressive if unappetising saga. To elaborate a little, one might add the testimony of that delightful character, Thomas Fresh, first Inspector of Nuisance under the new sanitary régime, whose quadrennial report of 1851 to the Health Committee on the workings of his Nuisance Department is interesting. His duties embraced lodging-houses, slaughter-houses, knackers' yards and smoke, cellar, and midden regulation. The police were used, in sanitation as later in school attendance, to conduct cellar censuses and other nuisance inquiries. 'Four intelligent and competent police officers' examined and measured every cellar in the borough for Thomas Fresh, and the tie-up of this with their more direct interest in crime is self-evident. It was Fresh who made prominent the serious problem of civic illiteracy. Thousands could not read the cellar-eviction orders, the midden-emptying application forms, the regulations posted in each lodging-house and slaughter-house and so on. The strain of civic illiteracy on the campaign for public education has never thoroughly been investigated, but it was a troublesome obstacle in an ever more complicated social context. In these opening years Fresh had anything up to a hundred complaints weekly to cope with and he inherited the hapless task of scouring streets after the inefficient subcontractors had passed by, and it was not until 1867 that the Council made all scavenging a public function. There was no regular dustbin clearance until 1900, although it had been estimated in the 1860s that, on any given day, there was always 64,000 tons of 'filthy refuse' in the borough.

Both Newlands and Fresh knew that the struggle was far from finished. Two major areas remained inviolate. One was that comprising the outlying districts, the swampy, thinly-populated townships without regulation which in some way threatened the town. Fresh gloomily pointed to five refuse and midden depots situated outside the borough bounds; the administrative inconvenience seemed to him to outweigh the geographical convenience. This menace was rather exaggerated, but it was a valuable argument for men like John Newlands, who was anxious to incorporate these outlying townships into the borough to unify and consolidate the sanitary format. The other area, a more serious obstacle, was housing. Public health was now much more positive, but it still fell foul of sacred property rights and the tough defences of landlordism. Newlands was prominent in drafting much of the 1854 Sanitary Amendment Act, which outlined a pro forma contract for house drainage at 6s a yard and introduced more stringent rules on such matters as cellars, domestic hygiene, air pollution and the demolition of insanitary property. But there were no real inroads made into housing until the 1858 Local Government Act, which included adoptive clauses in planning policy. Yet the Liverpool Land and House Owners' Association opposed these as it had opposed the whole sanitary programme and for six years it prevented the clauses being adopted locally as bylaws.

The private property problem was, for Newlands, one for the future. During the sixties some slight progress was made, but the striking feature was the dual advance of the newly completed Rivington Pike waterworks and the newly completed sanitary programme. They flourished in partnership so much that in 1872 an over-enthusiastic observer, not without bathos, felt moved to cry that 'the victory of the water-closet was now assured'. It would be another generation before a real dent was made in Liverpool's tragic death- and morbidity-rates. It was still hard to keep abreast of the problem as population continued to increase, but by 1860 Liverpool, in water-supply and sanitation as in social medicine, was regarded as an example to the nation of what could and what must be accomplished.

CHAPTER SEVEN

The early years of the Liverpool School Board

Today the Liverpool City Council controls, in varying degree, the fortunes of many educational establishments. In 1870 the council supervised but two schools, North Corporation and South Corporation, and even this was two more than any other municipal authority. These two schools had been opened as early as 1827 on an experimental basis. The Liberals had hoped to open an interdenominational school in each ward, but this ambition was scotched by the Conservative and Anglican opponents of the scheme. None the less, North and South Corporation schools were maintained, and the buildings are still in use today. Although the venture was not as happy as it might have been, no other council in England had organised any schools at all prior to 1870. Education was principally organised by the Church societies, who received grants-in-aid from the Committee of the Privy Council responsible for education. Grant-assisted schools were subject to inspection, and the state thus exerted some control through this financial lever, but before 1870 it did not initiate action in the education field.

One of the major reforms of Gladstone's first and most influential ministry was Forster's Education Act of 1870, which enabled the creation of School Boards, popularly elected local committees which would construct schools and supervise attendance and generally 'fill in gaps' left by the church schools. On 7 September 1870 the Liverpool council unanimously resolved that application should be made for the formation of a School Board and on 13 November the Privy Council Department of Education issued its precept for the election of a board. Numerous candidates were nominated and 'there appeared every prospect of a warmly contested election', according to the First Triennial Report of the School Board in 1873. The prospect alarmed rather than excited Liverpool worthies, and 'a large number of gentlemen' agreed on the then famous 'Liverpool platform'. This was aimed at healing the breaches among religionists. 'Religious instruction', the platform ran, 'should be permitted for the children of these parents who desire them to receive it, such religious instruction to be, so far as is practicable, in accordance with the wishes of the respective parents'. At a public meeting this tolerant proposal was adopt and a committee was formed to select fifteen candidates for uncontested election. It took the committee several meetings to decide on seven Anglicans, four Catholics and four Nonconformists, and the respective religious bodies chose their delegates: 'A combined list was agreed upon, and the remaining candidates were prevailed upon to ultimately withdraw.' This uncontested election was conducted 'at a cost to the ratepayers of only £33 12s 4d', the financial being presumably more important than the democratic consideration, and, immediately, one could see the total significance of the religious factor.

The board's first meeting was on 15 December. It was a sprightly start. Liverpool's was one of the earliest boards to be convened. Christopher Bushell, who had been prominent in the 'Liverpool platform' campaign, was appointed chairman and he proved to be a highly important figure in Liverpool educational circles. The Department of Education soon demanded a return of the existing educational provision, and the School Board showed some initiative in organising its own census under the auspices of Major Greig, the head constable, and twenty of his officers. It was a massive job, for Liverpool's populace was as fluid as it was sizeable, but the police completed their onerous task in six weeks. There were 109,000 children between 3 and 13 years of age, and of these 14,000 were middle- or upper-class, leaving 95,000 from the 'popular' classes for whom the 1870 Act was intended, of whom 38,000 were infants, that is under 7 years old.

A measurement of educational provision revealed a deficiency of 10,000 juniors and 17,000 infants. The imbalance was sharp. Whereas one junior in six might not expect to find a school place, for infants, it was one in two. The idea of beginning school at three sounds strange to modern ears, but it compensated, in theory, for the early school-leaving age. With some adjustments in terms of some districts having surplus places that could be deployed, the board finally plumped for a 22,000 deficiency. There were 80 public elementary schools, that is, in receipt of state grants, and these were made up of 47 Church of England, 16 Roman Catholic and 17 Nonconformist schools. There were 44 non-inspected schools, many of which were hopeful of becoming 'public' schools, and there were 14 miscellaneous schools—industrial schools, orphanages and the like—with an astounding collection of 99 private adventure schools, giving a total of 237 schools.

The report on these lines submitted to the department evoked a swift and firm response. A total of 17,000 places for which the board had taken credit were in private adventure and non-inspected schools which could not be recognised as efficient. Provided Liverpool addressed itself 'without delay to the arduous duties' of 'providing a large amount of school accommodation' their lordships of the Privy Council hoped 'no requisition will eventually be required'. In January 1872, a year after its first meeting, the Liverpool School Board decided to provide accommodation for 6,000 children, and this in spite of the departmental estimate of a 40,000 deficiency.

One is forced to speculate on the board's motivations. The town council had asked for a board before it had been forced upon it by the compulsory clauses of the Act. The department, in suspicious mood, had told the council that having a board did not 'supersede the necessity' for a district return and that to it belonged 'the ultimate responsibility of determining' any deficiency. Now the board was indulging in fanciful arithmetic with its optimistic inclusion of schools 'intending' to become efficient, of such unlikely institutions as the Working Men's Mission and the Seamen's Orphanage and of a hundred private schools, some of them with only eight scholars, and run by a gang of old dames, most of them Irish.

Had Liverpool thought that attack was the best form of defence? Did it try to beat the system by falling in with it before it was pushed, hopeful that state interference might be dodged? Liverpool had successfully avoided what it regarded as the worst excesses of national Poor Law control; perhaps now it was attempting the same kind of avoiding action. Certainly Liverpool felt itself capable of handling the situation. As late as 1903 a survey prepared by the Liverpool Education Committee argued that in 1870, 'Liverpool was one of the few large towns in which the provision made by voluntary effort was fully equal to the estimated requirements'. This independent streak, bordering on the introverted, possibly left the Liverpool authorities smug rather than dishonest, firm in the belief that Eliza Flint, with her handful of private adventure charges housed in No 2 Bright Street, was meeting Forster's call for stimulating 'the intellectual force of the individual'.

But the twilight mood of mid-century state intervention was changing, in many local eyes, to the sombre hue of much more effective central control. Quickly and gently threatening, the department countered each of the board's moves, easing it toward the national view of Liverpool's need. In the summer of 1872 it roundly condemned any acceptance of private schooling and announced that 21,000 places were required. The board was staggered by this request. It had hoped that its own scheme for 6,000 places, plus the constantly expanding effort, would have been sufficient. It did not recover from the shock until January of the following year when after 'long and careful consideration' and speaking in the name 'of a reasonable and just economy', the board once more pleaded its case.

It asked London to take into account 'the extreme poverty and migratory character of many thousands of the population, the precarious nature of their employment, and the temptations offered to parents to avail themselves of the great demand for the services of their elder children'. The Liverpool board pointed to the difficulties—'in their magnitude peculiar and local'—and asked for a less severe line from the central department. The board was still hopeful that some of the private schools would join the inspected list; it was equally hopeful that the department would accept high percentage deductions for absenteeism in its calculations. The board said that 74,000 children required educating and there were 62,000 places available, thousands of them not regularly used because of their inconvenient location. With proper district adjustment, the deficiency could be calculated at 15,400, of whom 12,000 were infants and not subject to the same obligatory rulings on attendance as the juniors. Of the intended 6,000 new places, 3,500 were for these remaining juniors, leaving 2,500 places and upgraded private schools to cater for the infants.

The department was as fast to query as the board was slow to reply. Barely a week passed before a stern letter arrived from London, which while accepting 'for a present estimate' the Liverpool calculations, pointed out that this in no way invalidated the overall deficiency in the borough, a deficiency, the department blandly reminded the board, daily widened by that expanding population over which the board so fussed. Another six months of 'numerous and prolonged sittings' passed. Emerging from its brown study in the summer of 1873, the board now discussed a school provision sub-committee report recommending the purchase of nine additional sites to accommodate nearly 7,000 more junior children. It also recommended that schools with excess junior places should be reorganised for infant work and it attacked the department's 'complete condemnation' of the private adventure system which the sub-committees held had many 'popular advantages'. Only by six votes to five did the board save the report from a six-month adjournment. For the first time a definitive split is seen between the hardliners wanting little rate expenditure and the moderates prepared to go some way to meet the department's wishes.

An outspoken petition from the Liverpool Land and House Owners'Association was lengthily discussed at the protracted debate on this report on 18 August. The memorial objected to the heavy weight of taxation with which the thrifty would be burdened for the benefit of feckless parents, and ultimately the report was adopted by ten votes to five. Again the department was quick to reply. Early in September it grudgingly approved the revised scheme.

Almost three years had passed. One or two new schools were already in existence, but the general scheme of Liverpool education took three years to resolve, with the department sharply counter-punching and the board resting quietly, as it were, between each round. Administrative delay, especially at a time when managerial techniques were raw, was inevitable, but in three years the problem had grown again. The board obviously longed for miracles of voluntary effort to lift Liverpool out of its slough of deficiency, and it is apparent that all the several forces—economic, political, and religious—were very delicately poised. It is interesting to pursue the tortuous negotiations of board and department as they jockeyed their way toward compromise. In effect, it was a 7,000 compromise between the department who wanted 19,000 new places and those members of the board who wanted none.

The actual provision of the new accommodation began with a search for sites to meet the initial call for 6,000 places, and by the end of 1872 six sites had been purchased for £11,000. E. R. Robson, the London School Board architect, was asked for his advice. He helped to revolutionize school architecture after his study of German building methods, and his active role in Liverpool's planning illustrates the enormous influence of the London School Board at this stage. Large schools with several departments, permitting of 'fine gradations' of classes, were proposed, with the now statutory 'triple classification' of infants, juniors, and seniors. The central hall system was used. Classrooms opened on to the 'principal school-room', as opposed to the older mode of one large schoolroom. A shrewd balance was struck. The single hall system had allowed for the direct control of pupil-teachers and assistant teachers by the imperious, ever-present schoolmaster or mistress. The central hall system offered some retreat and privacy from the packed house of earlier days, but ease of supervisory access was retained and 'upper panels of clear glass' were a feature of each classroom. Countless thousands have been and are being educated in this type of school building. The board also experimented, in futuristic vein, with a movable set of classrooms accommodating 600 children and these, from the set fee charged all age groups, were called the penny schools.

On sites and buildings, the board's loans and expenditure amounted to £63,000 during its first triennial period. It had little but empty sites and half-built premises to show for its tenure of office when the tri-yearly elections came round. The only board schools in operation were in temporary premises or were going concerns transferred to the board under the 1870 Act, and these included the North and South Corporation Schools and the Welsh Charity Schools in Russell Street, probably the most well known of Liverpool's old charity schools. These obviously added little to the overall accommodation.

The Liverpool School Board exercised a detailed control over these few schools both in curricular and managerial terms. The formation of boards of managers, grants for pupil-teachers, fees, alterations, salaries, 'holydays' and other elements in school life were rigorously supervised. The board also laid down syllabus carefully in the form of an administrative *diktat*. The authorized version of the Bible was to be daily read with 'such explanations and instructions in the principles of religion and morality as are suited to the capacities of children', but the Douai edition for

Roman Catholic children was not permitted as it constituted a distinctive 'religious formulary' contrary to the 1870 Act. The board failed to stress the conscience withdrawal clause of the Act and, in practice, all children were in receipt of daily biblical instruction. The board even wished a single hymnal, *Gems of Song*, on its schools. Other subjects were regarded as 'essential' and their compulsory syllabus and books were firmly outlined—these were the three 'R's', grammar, history, geography, vocal music, and drill. The teacher had little room for manoeuvre, hedged in as he or she was with local dictation and the inflexible national codes upon which, subject to inspection, the state grants rested.

The board interested itself in technical education. Henry Pooley led the campaign for science classes and 'a gentleman of practical attainments' was to be appointed as a peripatetic teacher. 'It is of great importance,' resolved the board, 'in a national point of view, to impart at least the elements of sound scientific knowledge to the future artisans of this country, in order, as far as possible, to qualify them to compete on equal grounds with the same classes in continental nations.' This sentiment would be equally at home in the 1970s.

Despite these brave activities, the first board disbanded with no new school opened and with only 3,000 pupils under its surveillance. In December 1873, after another agreement on candidates, the second board was elected without contest. These were new faces. One was Samuel Greg, who was to be one of the board's doughtiest stalwarts, the other was S. F. Rathbone, brother of William Rathbone and a member of that family renowned on Merseyside for its social commitment. He gave up his seat on the council and was immediately appointed chairman to the board. Samuel Rathbone built for himself a national as well as a local repute in educational circles, and only severe ill health prematurely curtailed his energetic contribution to the nation's educational development.

The first board had, however, resolved one vital issue; that of attendance control, which 'both in the eyes of the board itself and of the general public, appear to be its most important duty—to which its other labours, however important in themselves, are only subsidiary'. This honest avowal reinforces a point often missed, that the boards saw themselves as custodians of compulsory attendance rather than erectors of schools. There was never any difference of opinion among board members about this, and indeed Liverpool's were the first bylaws to receive Privy Council sanction in June 1871.

The bylaws were straightforward and standard. Children between five and thirteen were, with certain minor exceptions, obliged to attend school. Although a national ruling on compulsion came later, the action of local regulations enforced attendance in many areas soon after 1870, and by 1873 Liverpool had the surprisingly large number of twenty-six school visitors flushing out the truants. Litigation was heavy. In the first two years nearly 1,500 fines and 234 light terms of imprisonment were inflicted.

Despite its punitive zest, the board could only rally the attendance figures from 31,000 to 39,000. Amid the fluid, seething life of a great port, families came and went regularly, leaving no chance of checking on school attendance. The so-called 'street arabs' highlighted the problem. The police undertook a street census of these vagrant waifs and in a fortnight's 'picking up' nearly a thousand were investigated. To the board's astonishment it was discovered that this motley gang of shoe-blacks, rag-gatherers and other types of beggar were rarely orphaned or deserted, but merely supplementing the family income. The variegated pattern of dock-life threw up a host of possibilities for the enterprising youngster, but it was not many years past since Liverpool, like the other big cities, had reached the strange impasse where there was neither work (because of new regulations and new techniques) nor school for hundreds of children. Now the board was anxious to press home obligatory attendance. But fees still had to be paid and this became a crucial issue; impoverished parents could not afford to keep the law, and the board proposed to subsidise them. A howl of rage signalled the anger of the Nonconformists; where necessitous children attended board schools, they were happy, but where they attended church schools, they were outraged. It was nothing less than the subvention of organised religion from the rates. The board pointed out that the state already made grants to these schools but the Nonconformist faction thought it 'a singular doctrine' that these prior injustices might warrant further unjust acts. It was, they claimed, 'a retrograde step' providing for the 'inculcation of creeds and dogmas'. The friction was such that W. E. Forster had to intervene before the proposition was accepted.

The early years of the Liverpool School Board

Religion was as ever the critical feature. Two points are worthy of note. First, the Nonconformist support for the Bible-centred religious instruction of the board schools had a theological bent. Opposed as they were to ritual, the purportedly interdenominational scriptural story and hymn, which is still the base of many a school assembly, suited them, whereas the Anglicans and Catholics preferrred something a little more sacramental. Second, and of some significance, the board's premier function was attendance, and this throws a different light on the conventional view that School Boards and churches were locked in constant feud. When there were few board places, as in Liverpool, it was the board's task to force children into the church schools. The board members were all churchmen and in those early days it was their role to act as the public protector of the private sector of education. Attendance and the rote-learning begotten of attendance were the keys to the state grants that subsidised church schools. In turn, as long as the church schools could sustain their effort, the rates need not be unduly deployed for school building. The implication that board members were anti-clerical believers in a high education rate-levy is, of course, absurd. They were churchmen and ratepayers. In those first three years the board spent the equivalent of a $\frac{1}{2}$d rate; that is, 2d for every Liverpool resident, at a time when the Poor Law cost 6s and the police 4s a head.

Under the influence of Samuel Rathbone and others, the Liverpool School Board did improve on this somewhat unadventurous and unpropitious opening to its history. By 1880 the board controlled twenty-one schools, ten of them entirely or in part newly constructed. They were Queens Road (the first new board school, officially opened by W. E. Forster himself), Chatsworth Street, Roscommon Street, Ashfield Street, Butler Street, Beaufort Street, Walton Lane, Upper Park Street, Harrington and Clint Road. Most of them are still active today. They were then able to accommodate upward of 12,000 children. Average attendance jumped by 63 per cent to 51,000. The odd feature was that there were 23,000 board places and 76,000 inspected non-board places, a total of 99,000. Put another way, and allowing for a 10 per cent rise in population, ten years' endeavour had increased the ratio of pupils to population from one in sixteen to one in twelve. With well over half a million inhabitants, Liverpool might have expected to find more than 50,000 in its public elementary schools, especially as there were practically two places for each one of them.

What did the man in the street think of this latest attempt at governmental interference? Consumer reaction is difficult to assess at this distance of time, but the *Porcupine*, a rather solemn weekly in the Victorian tradition which enjoyed a respectable vogue in nineteenth-century Liverpool, provides some interesting comment. In 1877 a series of articles 'Education past and present' was published, the work of 'a Liverpool Shipwright', officially described by the editor as 'a bona-fide working-man' representing 'a class not sufficiently heard' on education questions. His articles reflected on the work of the Liverpool School Board in its formative period. He was hostile to the extreme Liberal and Nonconformist wing and the proletarian politicos, who, he shrewdly suggested, were 'aiming to reach the goal of their ambition, the cross benches of the commons, and to tack the magic initials to their names'. He was a friend of the Whig masters, Brougham and Lord John Russell, and of the established church with its 'well-won position as the educator of the youth of the country'.

Accepting these prejudices, his views made helpful reading. His biases were in any case not untypical of the upper echelons of the working-classes in late Victorian England, with their support for the Primrose League nationally and, locally in Liverpool, for the Orange Lodges. He accused the board plainly of manipulating its membership 'to protect the interests of your separate sects. One of you was elected because he happened to be a Welshman'. He saw clearly the 'wretched warfare' of sectarian controversy which was already crippling English education and has long continued to do so. In Liverpool he claimed it had produced a compromise board at a 'dull dead level of mediocrity'.

Examining the figures for 1876, he was not impressed; £5,000 had been paid for official staff, such as school visitors. Teachers' salaries at £11,000 were only double this amount, as if it took half the cost of teaching the children to ensure they were present and in good order. He accepted the £7,000 on fees, fuel, light, rent, and cleaning, but £16,000 on administrative and maintenance costs appalled him. Sarcastically, he set against the £330 for the school officer's uniforms the £74 for prizes for the board's 8,000 charges. The net total was £50,000—to manage 6 new, 8 transferred or leased and 2 temporary schools. Just over 8,000

Page 125   Everton Football Club, today

LEWIS & Cº CLOTHIERS & BOOTMAKERS

Page 126   Lewis & Co in its earliest days

children were in average attendance, and it was costing £8 per capita to educate them. 'A Liverpool Shipwright' compared this enterprise with 'the unceasing, oft-times unthankful, toil' of Liverpool's 'hard-working, poorly-paid clergy' and its other charitable educational agencies.

He next turned his attention to the board's building policy, which was 'utterly at variance with the wants of the town' in that it confined building operations to the outskirts of the town instead of its teeming centre. The board had justified this in terms of migratory population, but its *Porcupine* critic hinted that schools had been built in outlying areas 'for fear the denominationalists should occupy them'. He adverted to serious rumours about deficient construction—'the Queens Road schools are now notorious'—and the high cost of repairs. Apparently the workmen felt considerable jerry-building was being allowed. He insisted that the new schools were being 'erected for classes who are quite willing to pay for the benefits received', and that the board's efforts to anticipate demand had been unsuccessful and over-expensive. Board schools must not, he averred, be located 'where they compete with the efforts of the religious bodies'.

'A Liverpool Shipwright' reminded his readers that the shipping and allied trades were still in a depressed condition, with wages of 18s to 24s for a full week's work, and life 'one long grind for bread'. Christopher Bushell had advised parents to avail themselves of the savings banks in a time of prosperity that they might meet the advancing costs of their children's education without feeling the pinch. 'A Liverpool Shipwright' compared Bushell's savings banks with Marie Antoinette's famous advice, quaintly printed in the *Porcupine* as 'why did they not go to the confectioners and buy buns'. He longed for Earl Russell's scheme of free schools for the common people, with religious bodies providing any higher education at a personal expense. Finally, he implored the board to act forcefully in response to its 'crucial test', the reclamation of street arabs. He would have none of the board's technical explanations for their existence on the streets, nor would he accept that helping them 'would be paying a premium on parents' neglect'. In a progressive-sounding passage, he declared that the board should 'be not afraid of pauperising posterity' by helping those 'little outcasts' who had flown 'into the arms of that stony stepmother, the street'. It was a nonsense, he believed, to assume that the children would necessarily grow into adult paupers and idlers because their childhood had been spent in public care. Nor, he argued, should the parents be considered, for they were past reclaiming, and the board should concentrate on the children. It is still argued today that social welfare enfeebles and degrades, but 'a Liverpool Shipwright' was sensible enough to spot that children had no positive choices in the matter and should not 'be neglected because parents are drunken and vicious'. He suggested that reticence on the street arab issue arose from so many of the strays being Catholic, but he urged the board to override this petty difficulty and set up half a dozen refuges for these children.

However wild and exaggerated some of these accusations might have been, this rather erudite working-man's viewpoint raised several meaningful questions. The board was persisting in its policy of proportionate sectarian representations among its membership, and that certainly meant, as its critics indicated, a danger of self-cancelling and mediocre rule. His hints that the selection of school sites and the treatment of street arabs had religious motivations was assuredly different from the bland formalisms of the board's official records. There was and is substantial religious bitterness in Liverpool, and doubtless there was some truth in these oblique accusations. None the less, the board, even when it was not arranged to satisfy sectarian delegation, would inevitably be composed of denominationalists. The sometimes purported contest of school board versus church is a facile one. Secularists, let alone atheists, were rarely in a majority; most boards entirely consisted of Christians, and when antagonism occurred, it was often between church and church. If the Liverpool board was a balance of denominationalists, it would seem a contradiction to argue that board schools were being located to outflank denominationalists as a bloc.

As well as all board members being denominationalists, equally they were all ratepayers, and this was probably the very manner in which they and 'a Liverpool Shipwright' differed in status. If the new schools had been strategically placed and if the plight of the street arabs had been plausibly explained away, then financial rather than religious interest seems a safer interpretation. Schools built, like Queens Road, in districts where ratepayers resided could offer a direct service to those providing the money.

Street arabs obviously had no concern with rate payment, so their heartfelt pleas could be fobbed off. This is, of course, no less hypothetical than the shipwright's heavy hints of sectarian squabbles, but the economic interpretation does match the cautious unwillingness of the early boards to cut a dash or offend minorities.

The shipwright reserved some of his most venomous stings for the bureaucratic proclivity of the board. The board in 1876 spent £50,000 per year as opposed to an average of £9,000 in 1871-3, nearly five times as much in three years, with a hefty fraction devoted to managerial charges. The number of children under board supervision had only doubled, although, of course, brand-new schools were proving more expensive than hired and transferred ones. The process of managerial procreation, getting under way in the 1870s, was to reach astronomical proportions in the following century. The shipwright's solution was interesting, and not untypical of a number of commentators, for he suggested that public education should be organised like the general post office under the control of 'an educational Rowland Hill'. By this he presumably inferred that a national system was necessary, and that it should be run on businesslike lines like the GPO, which had speedily earned a high reputation in Victorian England. It was as if a modern observer might call for a Beeching or a Robens to rationalise some public service. In its own time it also echoed the cry for more centralisation of public control. Then as now, for instance, there were those wishing to see the police established as a national force. As in most of these other cases, education was to retain much of its local character and control, for the support for provincial supervision was intense and deep-rooted. The country, according to 'a Liverpool Shipwright', was 'paying dearly for its whistle', whereas the post office gave cheap and efficient service. This, with his laudatory remarks on the labour of love among voluntary educationalists, placed the shipwright on the side of those concerned for the moral rectitude of purchased education, an issue that was to become even more inflamed in later years.

It was perhaps this atmosphere which warned the Liverpool School Board to be a cautious and not a crusading body, one which made a virtue of its frugality. It had picked its way warily, concentrating on making existing arrangements more efficacious rather than on executing full-blooded plans of its own. The board had steered a tremulous course between the extremists, both national and local, between those eager for a massive, radical programme of school-board building and those who shuddered at the very thought of a penny piece being spent on education. Its compromising, procrastinating approach probably left the middle of the road ratepayer not too displeased. The board began to grow and extend. In 1903 the Liverpool Education Committee replaced the Liverpool School Board, and the multi-purpose corporation embraced the ad hoc elected board. By this time the board had control of 175 educational establishments of various kinds and of a system which touched on over 60,000 scholars. Its annual expenditure was now £165,000 and it employed, apart from well over 1,000 teachers, more than 100 attendance officers. The board's 49 public elementary schools were attended by 50,000 children, leaving another 80,000 to the voluntary system which supported upward of 100 schools. It was a complex organisation and one that had grown hugely in thirty years. Possibly its stable and pedestrian beginning helped, having perhaps provided a more stolid footing than a rumbustious adventure in educational high jinks. The Liverpool School Board was determined to walk before it ran.

CHAPTER EIGHT

Everton Football Club: the opening seasons

It is with some trepidation that one risks losing half the potential local readership by deciding to narrate the story of Everton, rather than Liverpool, Football Club. The justification of the author (himself a near-hysterical Manchester United supporter) is simply that Everton is older than Liverpool. Just as Cambridge was formed by a splinter movement from Oxford, so did Liverpool originate in a breakaway move from Everton. As the alumni of Cambridge would agree, age is no criterion of superiority. To be older can be preferable, as with wine, or not, as with chicken.

Football has an ancient history, reaching back to the days of Roman, Greek, and Chinese antiquity. It was well known in medieval Florence. In England it was a spontaneous folk-game for the farm boys in the countryside and the apprentices in the towns. Its anti-authoritarian tendencies are legendary. 'Footeballe', said Thomas Elyot, the Tudor educationist and author of *The Governour*, 'wherein is nothing but beastlie furie and extreme violence'. However, 'mob football' was disciplined through its introduction into the public schools and universities, thereby incidentally helping to reduce the sway of hunting and shooting. Under the influence of educators like Thomas Arnold, the character-building qualities of athletic sports were demonstrated, and by way of this 'muscular Christianity', football was to draw together the upper crust and the lower drawer of English society.

Sports were constantly performing this integrative function in the nineteenth century, much as the theatre had done in Tudor London. Horse-racing was an obvious example, while prize-fighters like Tom Cribb or Tom Sprigg found admirers among lords and commoners alike. Cricket was to exhibit the dichotomy most clearly with its distinct division, and yet balance, of professional and amateur. Liverpool was to see little of this, but over in

Manchester, the lordly A. C. Maclaren and his equally skilled professional counterpart J. T. Tyldesley were perfectly to illustrate this consummation for Lancashire and England.

Before Everton was formed, the game had had to rationalise itself. In rural meadows and schools handling and hacking were the traditions, whereas in the constricted environs of the towns, dribbling and passing had developed. Outside London, Sheffield was the leading centre. The Old Harrovians, who started the Sheffield club, so disapproved of handling that they provided their rustic opponents with white gloves and florins to hold in an attempt to deter them. Cambridge University and F. C. Thring, the headmaster of Uppingham, gave a lead in rule-making, and in October 1863 the Football Association was formed. Then began the great debate on rules. Hacking was the critical point. Mr Campbell of Blackheath saw in hacking, as many did in boxing, the true testing-ground of masculinity and English character. Protesting at its proposed abolition, he said 'it savours more of the feelings of those who liked their pipes or grog or schnapps more than the manly game of football', and he offered 'to bring over a lot of Frenchmen who would beat you with a week's practice'. This chauvinistic objection was dismissed, handling as well as hacking was ruled out, the chasm between the two sides was unbridgeable, and in 1871 the Rugby Union was formed.

A year previously a Sunday school had been opened in St Domingo's Vale in North Liverpool, representing the Methodist New Connexion which had flourished in Liverpool since the last decade of the previous century. In the heartland of the Orange and Papist feud, football, the secular religion of Liverpool, was suckled at the bosom of Nonconformity. Oliver Cromwell, one of Nonconformity's favourite sons, had anticipated a much later Oxbridge tradition by failing to take a degree whilst at Sydney Sussex College, Cambridge, because, it was said, of his attachment to football. If time-lines could weave concentric patterns, one might recall Prince Rupert training his artillery on a besieged Liverpool in the Civil War but a few yards from Everton's headquarters. He might mentally have pencilled in Cromwell as a stopper centre-half.

As with the schools so with the churches. They were anxious to save their urban parishioners from the degeneracy of town life, and wholesome games provided an opportunity. The Sunday school in St Domingo's Vale soon started a cricket team, and in 1878, Hegirah for the purist Evertonian, a football team was started. Two families, the Wades and the Cuffs, had been prominent throughout the history of New Connexion Methodism (one of several offshoots of Wesleyan Methodism, which suffered one or two mild schisms toward the end of the eighteenth century). Appropriately, Arthur Riley Wade and W. C. Cuff figured in that first football side. Football flourished and almost immediately, in 1879, the name of Everton was adopted.

The universities and top schools had made their mark with such teams as Cambridge and Oxford Universities, the Wanderers, Old Etonians, Old Harrovians, and, both with Harrovian connections, Sheffield and Epping Forest. One of football's earliest stalwarts, Arthur Kinnaird, played in nine cup finals in ten years for Old Etonians and the famous Wanderers. Next, the evangelical mood passed to the churches. It was an age insistent on saving the poor through good works—the Salvation Army was formed in the same year as the Football Association. Fitness was all the rage, and from mid-century on hygiene consciousness advanced remarkably, and cleanliness was inseparable from godliness. From the cold-water baths and cross-country runs of the public school and the enthusiastic athleticism of Thomas Hughes or Charles Kingsley to the stirring message of Darwin's survival of the fittest and the sudden eruption of the temperance movement, health became a supreme goal.

St Domingo's Sunday school was only one of several local religious establishments to favour soccer—a characteristic university abbreviation—for St Peter's, St Benedict's, St John's, Bootle and Our Lady's, St Domingo Road, all looked to football to succour the welfare of youth. Municipal parks were becoming available for games, especially since the Public Health Act of 1848 had suggested 'public walks' for 'the humbler classes'. Everton was not the only clerical foundation to play its way into the higher echelons. Aston Villa started as a Wesleyan chapel team; Wolverhampton Wanderers grew up from St Luke's Church, Blackenhall; and a West Kensington Sunday school witnessed the origins of Fulham.

It was a struggle to maintain an interest in football on Merseyside, where there was a strong preference for rugby, still manifest in the quintet of top-class rugby clubs in the area. R. E. Lythgoe, who had been secretary of a southern team, the Druids, was the chief protagonist on behalf of soccer in Liverpool and an influential figure in the county at large. His Bootle side were Everton's main rivals. After Everton's first game under that name against St Peter's two days before Christmas 1879, the side met Lythgoe's Bootle in the following February. Apart from Bootle the local competition was frail, probably because middle-class support was lacking. In some places grammar schools had taken the hint from the public schools, and Blackburn Rovers and Leicester City are but two clubs which began life as grammar school 'old boys'. Teachers themselves ran teams, and Sunderland was originally the Sunderland and District Teachers' XI. Even board schools took up the game seriously, and Queen's Park Rangers has its origins partly in a board school team. But this was not happening in Liverpool.

So, for some years, local success was not sustained further afield. In Lancashire Association games Everton was often heavily defeated. In 1880 Great Lever beat them 8–1 and they lost the following year 13–1 to Bolton Wanderers. In these early years J. W. Clarke, landlord of 'The Queen's Head,' was secretary, and he kept an eye scoured for promising juniors from the local church teams like United Church Club, or from youth sides like the Stanley Parkists. Conflict with Bootle was not confined to the playing arena, for there was ugly talk of 'enticements'. Both clubs made counter-accusations of poaching among these junior sides. In 1882 Everton beat Bootle 4–1 before a 500-strong crowd, and soon after they began Saturday afternoon exhibition games in Stanley Park which sometimes attracted well over a thousand spectators. The next season, tempers were so inflamed that the players walked off during the heated local derby. 'Tricky Bootle', said the Everton fans, 'where the bugs wear clogs and fly backwards to keep the dust out of their eyes'. This foreshadowed the dreadful happenings of 1886 when the crowd broke up the Bootle-Everton clash in the first round of the Liverpool cup. The mid-twentieth century has no monopoly of football hooliganism.

The youth policy and the publicity of exhibition matches began to bear fruit. In 1883 Everton won the Liverpool Cup by defeating Earlstown. In those times there were two umpires as well as a referee, and one wonders at the implications, after this final, of a special vote of thanks to the Everton umpire. The 'Moonlight

Dribblers', as Everton were somewhat romantically nicknamed because of their habit of nocturnal training, had several notable players by now. Bob Morris was a noted tackler, and Tom Marriot was feared for his 'lunges'; George Bargery, late of Accrington, kept goal competently, while the leading goal-scorers were Provan and James McGill. McGill joined Everton in 1880 from Glasgow Rangers, Everton's first Scot, and the introduction to a Caledonian tradition that has persisted to the contemporary era of 'the golden vision', Alec Young.

The Gaelic migration began about this time. It was led by two Partick players, James Lowe and Fergus Suter, and there were many Scots anxious to play for clubs in the north of England, where employment was more readily obtainable than in Scotland. They introduced a more astute tactical insight and that accurate passing for which Scotland's football has always been famous. It led to something of a turning-point in the game, for the ascendancy of the south and its public school-orientated sides was now challenged by the northern artisans. The gauntlet was dramatically flung down when Darwen, in 1879, took the stylish Old Etonians to a second replay in the fourth round of the FA Cup.

It was now that the industrial and urban aspects of the game began to make themselves felt. Present-day football was very much moulded by industrialism, even though its substance was initially upper-class, and it is this volte-face which in some part justifies the worn chestnut about a gentleman's game for ruffians. Introduced into the populous districts to protect the health and sublimate the latently sinful energies of urban youth, football now became more and more a reflection of Victorian urban life. Sometimes it was straightforward enough. Factories and other commercial enterprises organised teams, perhaps, as is said of the brass bands of mills and mines, to distract the workers from thoughts of industrial agitation. Manchester United was originally Newton Heath Loco and, as early as 1863, North Staffordshire Railways commenced what was to become the history of Stoke City. Here there was an interesting balance, for Old Carthusians helped float the club.

However, it was more in the spectator element that industrialism and urbanism seemed most significant as there slowly emerged the zealous support for the town team by workmen enjoying a weekly respite from the rigours of their everyday employ. Vicariously and overtly they experienced the high triumph and low depression of the team's success and failure—they experienced this in the huge communion of the crowd, as in turn the clubs responded by an increasing emphasis on improved performance. Soon there began to appear that symbolic artefact of the industrial town; the football ground, its high stands and terraces crowded in and cramped by closely-built rows of artisan housing. Gone for ever were the open meadows and wide terrains of the Elizabethan village game. Just as the demographic explosion constrained practically every other social agency, it forced football into its small plot surrounded by tightly packed hordes of spectators. It is said, similarly, that the Chinese concentrate on table-tennis as the national sport because so many can participate in minute spaces.

Something of the sort seems prevalent in city life down the ages. The Nike Riots which, in sixth-century Constantinople, almost cost Justinian his imperial title, were sparked off by the passionate rivalry between the supporters of the two gladiatorial factions, the blues and the greens. Doubtless the Latin equivalent of ee-ay-addio rose from *hoi polloi* at Rome's Coliseum. The Kop is a constant in urban society. Indeed, many commentators believe that the proxy aggression of a Liverpool–Everton or a Rangers–Celtic match has drained off the adrenalin that might have been diffused into political or social rebellion.

These developments were coming, and Everton kept pace with them. The exhibition games on Stanley Park aside, Everton had an enclosed ground from 1882 on Cruitt's Field, Priory Road. In 1884 Cruitt grew tired of football on his field, and the club transferred to Orrell's Brewery Field at Walton. Here they developed the Anfield Road ground. At this juncture a shudder must surely run down the spine of every right-minded Everton fan, for this was later to be the home of Liverpool AFC—it was as if the Cardinal Archbishop had started life in a mosque. In 1885 the first game was played at the new premises, its enclosure capable of housing several thousand spectators, and Earlstown Borough were decisively swept aside to the tune of 5–0. Soon superior fixtures were negotiated against famous clubs like Blackburn Rovers, Blackburn Olympic, Accrington, and Bolton Wanderers. It was Blackburn Olympic who had finished the trail blazed by Darwen, and they were the north's first FA Cup-winners, beating

Old Etonians 2–1 in 1883. Three weavers, two spinners, an iron-foundryman, a plumber and a dentist's assistant were in the side.

The growing business interest in soccer was demonstrated at Everton by the activities of John Houlding, landlord of the Sandon Hotel which, by now, had replaced 'The Queen's Head' as the club's unofficial headquarters. This wealthy publican was active politically. He was on the Board of Guardians, he was a councillor who was to become mayor of Liverpool, and a busy member of the Liverpool Working-men's Conservative Association. He was known as King John of Everton. Apart from a shrewd eye for the profitable aspects of football, his keen political brain noted with delight the electoral popularity awaiting a successful soccer tycoon. It was just at this time that Major William Sudell was attempting to realise his proud boast to make Preston North End the 'invincibles', and financial interests were beginning to touch the game at several points. It is of interest to recall that Houlding's lieutenants were Sam Crosbie and Frank Brettle, the headmaster and one of the staff at Prince Edwin Street School, and A. Boylett, still steadfastly maintaining his family's connection with St Domingo's Sunday school. Sam Crosbie was a zealous fund-raiser and Frank Brettle, a one-time secretary of the club, had been a forward in Everton's very first line-up. In the conjunction with these men of education, church and business, the major influences not only in Everton's but in football's fortunes generally were personified.

By far the most significant factor in industrialism's effect on association football was the arrival of professionalism, and as the spectator angle grew, the professionalisation of football and of other sports developed. In the mid-1880s Accrington and Preston North End were in serious trouble; Accrington was expelled, and Major Sudell astounded the FA by proclaiming Preston's deliberate use of professionals to build his famous 'lilywhites'. Peter Parkinson of Bolton Wanderers led the short-lived British Football Association for professional teams. The amateur/professional controversy was almost as tense and critical as the earlier soccer/rugby debate.

C. W. Alcock, the FA secretary, much as he personally admired the amateur attitude, read the omens aright. Payments were being made, and nothing would stop the practice; better to control it, then, than force it underground. 'Veiled professionalism is the evil to be repressed,' said Alcock. In 1885 professionalism was legalised under certain limitations. Everton's first three registered professionals were George Dobson, from Bolton Wanderers, George Farmer, an ex-Oswestry player, and Alec Dick, late of Kilmarnock. Everton were soon in trouble over their professionals —the club was refused admission for a season to the Lancashire Cup because of its overfondness for professionals, and Lythgoe and the Liverpool Association, of which he was still the most prominent member, were also annoyed. They grew angry enough to remove the Liverpool Cup, which Everton had won three times in four years, from its place of honour in the Sandon Hotel. 'Gone but not forgotten' was the mourning text that replaced it. The strangest incident, however, concerned Everton's tryst with Bolton Wanderers in the FA Cup competition of 1887. Bolton won 1–0, but Everton protested that Bolton, pioneers of the professional game, had exceeded the regulations for paid players. After two drawn replays, Everton won the fourth game 2–1, and this time Bolton protested. Everton were found to have seven paid players, but three were on amateur registration to meet the FA ruling on professionalism. Everton (who by the time of the hearing had already lost to Preston in the next round) were suspended for a month. The gates for these games, incidentally, were touching 7,000, a crowd plenty of third and fourth division clubs would avidly welcome today.

By now football was well established in Liverpool. In 1883 and 1889 international matches against Ireland had their venue in Liverpool, the one at Aigburth, the other on Everton's ground. Thus far Everton had had little success in the FA Cup, indeed, on one regrettable occasion in 1886 the club miserably shirked a cup encounter with the redoubtable Glasgow Rangers. W. C. Alcock, most influential of football administrators, was responsible for the brilliant concept of cup football, and the FA Challenge Cup was first fought for in 1871. Like so much in soccer, it had a public school origin, for Alcock had remembered the success of the Harrow Cock House competition.

It was William McGregor, another notable administrator, who produced the twin for Alcock's cup, namely, the Football League. Everton were founder members along with Aston Villa, Preston North End, Accrington, West Bromwich Albion, Wolverhampton Wanderers, Blackburn Rovers, Burnley, Notts County, Stoke

City, Derby County, and Bolton Wanderers. The northern and midland hegemony was complete. No club south of Birmingham appeared in the first Football League and the fulcrum of soccer had moved absolutely. Six of these dozen founders are at present in the first division. Then as now Everton were able to guarantee good amenities, including a grandstand and regular attendance; these were the sureties which the league required.

On 8 September 1888 Everton played their first league match before a handsome gate of 9,000, and having undergone extensive training, they defeated the strong Accrington side 2–1. They were captained during the season by Nick Ross, late of Preston North End, who earned the then princely sum of £10 a month. This competent full-back was transferred back to Preston in the close season. His tenure of office had not been too exciting, for Everton finished a poor eighth in the first league tables, having scarcely gained an away point—what the *Liverpool Review* called the 'Everton Football Fiasco'.

In that close season a refurbished committee worked hard to rectify Everton's lack of offensive penetration. Chadwick joined them from Blackburn Rovers, and later he became the first Evertonian to don England's colours, playing in six internationals between 1891 and 1897. He formed a gifted left wing with Milward, who also won a couple of caps. Fred Geary, a centre-forward from Notts County, joined with them in putting the accent firmly on attack. The forceful Lata, a Scottish international, also joined the club and, the following year, two Third Lanark stars, Lockhead and McFarlane, contributed to the strong Celtic flavour of the Everton eleven. Jimmy Holt, a small Blackburn-born centre-half, widely admired for his 'cleverly illegal' tactics, steadied the defence. This reformation certainly had the desired consequence. Villa were mercilessly hammered 7–0, and it was reported that the Aston Villa stalwart, Archie Hunter, suffered a fit, so nonplussed was he at this grave indignity. Twenty thousand turned out to watch the game against 'Proud Preston', who easily held off the upstart challenge, winning 5–1. Still, Everton were second. And then, in season 1890–1, they became the Football League's third champions. It was a well-drilled side, tough, but, especially on the left flank, skilful in attack. The grand names of Preston, Villa, and Blackburn Rovers had to hide their astonishment and dismay as best they might.

This upsurge of success was as rewarding to Everton as it was startling to their rivals, and it was no temporary aberration. These two successful championship years heralded a purple patch for Everton, which for nearly twenty years remained one of England's leading sides. At a time when there were only the home internationals, with caps consequently much rarer than in the present era of a constant interchange of national fixtures, Everton mustered probably a dozen capped players in the nineteenth century. J. D. Robertson was capped sixteen times for Scotland at half-back.

The club was, however, first to undergo the ordeal of schism, and it was John Houlding who prepared the crucible of fire. In September 1891 he tried to form the Everton club into a limited liability company, and he prefaced this move by the shrewd purchase of a substantial piece of land adjacent to Anfield Road. Houlding was not popular in all circles. He had been blamed for Everton's lamentable performance in the first league season, and like many another abrasive and ambitious politico, he aroused plenty of enmity. There was widespread suspicion of his motives, and a solicitor, George Mahon, and W. R. Clayton, both Everton committee-men, opposed him. Feelings became inflamed, harsh threats and abuse were bandied, while the press took a somewhat excitable interest and Houlding was berated for his self-centred political and financial motivations. Simply, it was felt he wanted to complete and secure his dictatorial position in Everton's affairs. At a meeting 500 strong, only 18 signified in favour of John Houlding. His stranglehold on the land, however, necessitated a move.

It was a clean break, physical and personal. As Everton cut their links with King John, they moved from the south to the north side of Stanley Park, where they made Goodison Park their world-famed headquarters. Dr J. C. Baxter, one of the new brooms on the committee, contributed much of the fiscal backing. The 30,000 square yards of Goodison were purchased for £8,000, no small sum in the 1890s. Baxter, whose family were to enjoy a lengthy connection with Everton, assisted the club to establish itself as a limited company, a business transaction being undertaken by several leading clubs. It indicated the compelling commercial factor of big-time football, but in Everton's case it enabled the club to shake off the dominion of Houlding with whom the post-1888 committee had had no more than an uneasy relation.

Everton Football Club: the opening seasons

With a nostalgic backward glance, the ground was opened in August 1892 by that most frequent of cup finalists, Lord Kinnaird, and a week later, in the opening match, Everton beat Bolton Wanderers 4–2. Jardine, Howarth, Dewer, Boyle, Holt, Robertson, Lata, Maxwell, Geary, Chadwick, and Milward were the hallowed first to tread that adored turf. To celebrate further, the coming February witnessed Everton's very first triumph over Preston, a stylish victory to the tune of 6–0.

It was at this point that John Houlding started the Liverpool club with the aid of John McKenna, a native of County Monagghan. The first Derby game was in 1893. For prestige reasons and because they had another fixture, Everton turned out a mixed and weakened side which was beaten by the only goal for the Liverpool Cup.

Everton soon reclaimed the public's attention in the brightest of fashions when in 1893 they reached their first FA Cup Final. Everton had not enjoyed much success in this premier competition, and this was in fact the twenty-first in the series. Everton were represented by much the same team that celebrated the opening of Goodison; Williams for Jardine in goal; Kelso and Stuart for Dewer and Robertson in the defence, and Gordon for Geary at inside-left were the only changes. There was a characteristically Scots element in the composition of the side, which compared radically with their opponents, Wolverhampton Wanderers, who were known as the all-English eleven. They were not the favoured team, but, however prettily the Everton ball-players weaved their patterns, the forthright Wolves scored a goal and hung on grimly to their lead. It was a disappointment. Some argued that the players were distracted by the incredible crowd scenes, and indeed the game, played at Fallowfield, Manchester, was before a huge record crowd estimated at 45,000. There were difficulties in access and exit from Fallowfield, as well as an unprecedented issue of crowd control during the game. For that age, 45,000 was a fantastic gate, both sides having whipped up considerable public support, fans pouring in from Liverpool and Wolverhampton in a variety of transport. It was this game which led to the erection of strong fencing and walls around the field of play, the use of crush-barriers and much of the other paraphernalia of crowd supervision. Next year the Cup Final was played, for the first time, at Goodison Park before a crowd of 37,000, but it was widely felt that the dangers and troubles of the previous years had frightened off hundreds of other would-be spectators.

In the same year the first Derby between Liverpool and Everton in the first division was negotiated at Goodison Park. There was a 44,000 gate, a league record at the time. Everton won 2–0. By now Everton had justly won a reputation for fast and clever play, and the balance-sheets as well as the playing results looked healthier every year. In 1897 Everton again reached the Cup Final, but the club was once more doomed to frustration. Aston Villa, those indefatigable cup-fighters, sank Everton's hopes with a 3–2 victory. Bell and Boyle scored Everton's first-ever Cup Final goals. The tie was played at the Crystal Palace, and again there was a record crowd, this time of 65,000—a far cry from the January day of 1882 when 500 spectators watched Everton win their first Liverpool Cup. The mounting thousands who watched these games are as indicative of the growing stature of football as any other feature.

The FA Cup was an elusive prize. It was ten years before Everton battled through to another final at the Crystal Palace. This time their ambition was achieved against their opponents, Newcastle United, another team reputed for its cup-fighting qualities, in a closely contested game which Everton won 1–0. And there was Lord Kinnaird to present the cup to Everton. Everton were to reach the final the following year, only to suffer a third disappointment, this time a 2–1 defeat at the hands of Sheffield Wednesday. It had been a golden era, nevertheless, for Everton. They had helped found the Football League; they had been Football League champions, and then at the third attempt, the long-cherished summit of a Cup Final win was attained.

The names of that cup-winning side have a more familiar ring to the soccer enthusiast than the Bargeries and Chalks of the eighties: Scott, Crelley and Balmer; Makepeace, Taylor, and Abbott; Sharp, Bolton, Young, Settle, and Hardman. The suspicious Evertonian might start a little to find a Balmer in the side (Jackie Balmer was to skipper Liverpool in seasons much nearer the present) but the princely Elisha Scott is a name to conjure with. He played for both Everton and Liverpool, and, with Sam Hardy, another uncannily watchful Everton goalkeeper, he is always mentioned among the half-dozen or so most illustrious goalkeepers. Sharp, the outside-right, recalls the great service

Page 143
Owen Owen
now

Page 144 (*Above*)
Florence Maybrick;
(*right*) George Wise

given Everton by his family to the present age, when Jack Sharp, his son, is chairman of the club. Harry Makepeace, at right-half was one of a rare band to win a cup medal and score a century for England—he was a sterling opening bat for Lancashire and England, and later became the county coach.

Everton had achieved a considerable success in their first thirty years. Like most clubs, they were to have their frail patches, but the contemporary side of Alan Ball, Joe Royle and company need not and does not shrink from comparison with the far-off giants like Scott and Chadwick and Milward. And the interwar years were to be splendidly enlivened by the exhilarating and cheerful talent of Dixie Dean, who scored 379 goals between 1925 and 1938, including a record haul of 82 in season 1927-8.

Football is the most fluid of games, open to a permutation of interpretations and evolutions that is wellnigh inexhaustible. It is a restless, youthful sort of game, its fluent scope allowing for a ceaseless pattern of change, running a wide gamut of traits from the poetic to the brutal. Thirty years of football history is a long, long time. As well as reflecting the changing social character of the game and as well as exhibiting its own swift climb to excellence and success, Everton's first thirty or so years also witnessed quite amazing alterations in the nature of the sport.

The meadow pitch where the Everton saga began would have been roughly the same size as the Goodison Park playing area, although not so tenderly nurtured. There should have been corner flags, but no halfway lines, circles, or areas marked. The goals were approximately as wide as today, but cross-bars were unknown for, as in rugby, height was immaterial. It was in the 1870s before a tape 8ft high universally did service for a bar, and in 1891 Broadie produced his sensational goal nets.

It was as late as 1904 that knickerbockers had by law to cover the knees. Everton's first players would have also worn strong walking boots, tight jerseys and the tasselled cowls from which the idea of winning 'caps' developed. A team would wear the same styled headgear; hence, on international selection, one not only won but wore one's cap. The 1867 *Handbook of Football* rather naively thought it 'a good plan' for teams to have different colours. The writer had often, he averred, witnessed players, having hacked or tackled a colleague, declare, 'I beg your pardon, I thought you were on the opposite side'. Teams assuredly adopted a bizarre collection of fashions which belay the Victorian's reputation for drabness. They would certainly look more at home in the King's Road, Chelsea, than at Stamford Bridge. Sheffield Norwich paraded themselves in violet and black jerseys with a violet, blue, and yellow cap; Sheffield Mackenzie were resplendent in pink shirts and plaid bonnets; Hackney Black Rovers wore the somewhat sinister garb of black jerseys with a white skull and cross-bones on the chest; Aldenham School contrasted the simplicity of all-white jerseys with the stunning stroke of wearing black velvet turbans.

Everton were no slouches in the matter of gay, insouciant apparel. Blue and white stripes (plus other stripes according to choice) soon made way for black with a red sash, and then salmon jerseys and blue knickers. Ruby shirts with blue trimmings was the next choice. Either of these would now be guaranteed to evoke caustic and ribald commentary from the Gwladys Street end of Goodison Park. Later they settled for the more restrained blue and white quarters which eventually gave way to today's famous royal blue. The garish appearance of Everton and many of their opponents must have produced a kaleidoscopic illusion as play flitted from end to end.

Field of play and clothing were, however, peripheral to the principle reforms going on in the very basis of soccer. Several in Everton's earliest ranks must have known the game in the sixties when the eleven players comprised no less than nine forwards and two 'behinds', as the defenders were rather ambiguously termed. It was 1865 before the goalkeeper was introduced, although he still wore the same dress as his colleagues. Now there were eight forwards, and the two 'behinds' were happily retitled back and goal-cover. By 1870 there were moves to reduce the oversubscribed forward line to seven, and have no half-backs. When Everton began their career they were to employ a goalkeeper, two full-backs, two half-backs and six forwards. It was 1883, the year of Everton's first Liverpool Cup triumph, that the more familiar pattern of two full-backs, three half-backs and five forwards deployed in the long-standing 'W' formation was inaugurated. Now the pendulum has swung still further to the flexible formats of the 1960s, with 4–2–4 and 4–3–3 and similar permutations, all with a purported emphasis on a more total commitment of each player both to attack and defence.

Everton Football Club: the opening seasons

Why was the formation changed almost completely? It is argued that changing rulings and improved attacking ploys placed a greater responsibility on defensive attitudes, although needless to say, there was and has been no bar to more efficient defence techniques. It is a most radical change from no goalkeeper and nine forwards to the massed, marshalled defences of today, with entire teams cramped in their own penalty area and often a minimum of one or two front-runners. It might only be half a joke to secure a sociologist or historian of manners to examine the phenomenon and see something of the positive assurance of the Victorian 'top' nation in the former and a little of the vacillating caution of the twentieth century in the latter.

Certainly the game changed radically, mainly in terms of a dilution of its rugby tradition. Much had happened prior to Everton's inauguration. Control by hand and the 'fair catch' and mark, rewarded by a free kick, had not long been abandoned. It was an energetic pastime; if the ball crossed the lines, a frantic chase, in the lacrosse style, ensued in order to win the touch-down and subsequent throw-in, which, à la rugby, had to be right-angular. A goal-kick had to be earned in the same arduous manner, and if an attacker touched down behind the bye-line, he gained the splendid opportunity of a free-kick fifteen yards in front of the goals at the point where the ball crossed the line. The rugger offside rule was used, which meant the forward pass was illegal. This must have meant an easing of the defenders' problems. In 1867 three defenders between the attacker and the goal put the player on-side, and four years later the goalkeeper was permitted to use his hands.

When Everton played their first game against St Peter's, the cross-bar was permitted and the odd business of changing ends after each goal had only just been stopped. In their opening seasons throwing-in in any direction was legalised and, later still, the two-handed throw was introduced. Slowly, the rugby conventions—touchdowns, catches, throw-ins and so on—were removed, as Everton matured towards their founder membership of the Football League.

The overall flow of the game changed drastically in part as the rules changed and in part as the game itself forced alterations. At first sight an early Everton game would, as a spectacle, have appeared strange to the modern supporter. Sinuous dribbling was the order of the day, as in an apparently egocentric manner, each player embarked on a mazy dribble, tempting and avoiding as many tackles as possible, with one or two team-mates in support to pick up the loose ball and depart on the same course. It was a very highly developed sophistication of the forward rush in rugby. Nor should one be misled by the exotic apparel and the stern, stilted photographs of yesteryear. Men like McGill and Provan were very skilled dribblers indeed, and Everton were notable contributors to the art in the early 1880s.

Just as Everton's story opened, football was delicately poised between the pretty dribbling of the sixties and seventies, met, as it inevitably was, with fierce, crushing tackling, and the more open passing game. Assisted by the fundamental adjustment of the offside rule, the concept developed of parting with the ball quickly and accurately to team-mates more strategically placed. Scotland was truly the home of the passing game, which was obviously the critical change in the pattern of soccer. Everton, with its long line of Scottish professionals, pioneered the passing game, whilst maintaining the dribbling competence of men like Milward and Chadwick. With the Scotland 'cap' Lata, possibly the ablest performer, it was this well-drilled and forceful passing of Everton which took them into the Football League, to its championship and to the highest echelons of English and, eventually, European football.

Social historians have perhaps underestimated the inter-relation of sport and society. In G. O. Trevelyan's classic *English Social History* only two very minor references to football are included, but there are many Liverpolitans who would testify that football, either at Goodison Park or Anfield Road, has played as rich a part in their lives as the more usual fodder of social description.

CHAPTER NINE

The retail revolution: David Lewis and Owen Owen

The economic might of Liverpool has been reported and analysed at great length and with great skill. The contest of Mersey and Dee, the American slave trade, the busy cotton port and maritime agency for a score of industries, the Leeds–Liverpool canal and the Manchester Ship Canal, the Liverpool–Manchester railway and the wholesale development of communications, the vast extension of Liverpool's dockland, the seat of huge shipping and trading concerns—these and other significant stories tell the tale of Liverpool and its expanding economy.

One factor has not had such intense coverage. The retail trade, not just in Liverpool but throughout the country, has been far from overworked by the economic and social historians. Business history is a relatively new branch of historical research, but, even so, few retail concerns have been considered as against the more numerous accounts of commercial houses and industrial enterprises. Scarcely any economic or social history textbook mentions the topic, and while production and consumption figure largely, somehow distribution has been obscured. Marks and Spencer have had their biographer and, in a highly reputable pioneer work, Asa Briggs examined the 100-year growth of Lewis's. Commenting on the rarity of distributive history, he ruefully recalls the gibe about England being a nation of shopkeepers. Somehow the desire to record the life and work of these shopkeepers has been overshadowed by other themes. Some retailers claim that selling, however important, has come to be less well-respected than the honest, sturdy toil of production and is regarded as a trifle unsavoury and shaming, but the retail trades probably form the United Kingdom's largest source of employment today, and like it or not, retail distribution is the key to the smooth running of the economy.

In the nineteenth century retail marketing underwent as remarkable a change as industry itself and the change was needed in order to keep in gear with the revolution in production. In answer to the quickened flow of mass production and the heightened consumer demands of a swiftly growing population, the retail trade began its own corresponding revolution. Its principle was the large-scale, low profit operation; its base was the department store in which diversified retailing could come under the focus of one roof. The department store remains today the centrepiece of city retailing but of course the chain store and the supermarket, especially for foodstuffs, have developed alongside it and are by their nature capable of much greater geographical diversity. In general the retail trade is always a little behind the productive trades. This is partly because it does, obviously, follow production in practice and, in many instances, the two aspects had at one time shared common ground—the tailor, the milliner, the baker, and the butcher are straightforward examples of this. Part of the process of mass productivity was to separate manufacture from retailing, but then an equally obvious fact took over, which was simply that whereas only one or two centres for manufacture were required, distributive agencies had to be widely spread. Thus, initially, small-scale shopkeepers changed their role rather than disappeared; the shoeshop, for instance, came more to rely on wholesale suppliers than on cobbling on the premises. Compared with the manufacturing industries, there are still quite a number of self-employed and family concerns in the services sector of commerce.

It was indeed as late as the second half of the last century before the retail revolution was under way, some hundred years after the normally accepted beginnings of the industrial revolution. In 1861 John Wanamaker opened his store in Philadelphia; in 1852 Aristide Boucicaut floated the famed Bon Marché venture in Paris which was to have so many imitators. In England H. C. Harrod began that most elegant of department stores in 1849 and in 1863 William Whiteley, the Universal Provider, started his well-known business.

Liverpool had in these years by no means shrugged off its shroud of poverty, squalor, and deprivation. In some ways it was hardly a city in need of new-fangled experiments in marketing, but, by other tokens, the time was ripe. Standards were beginning to rise and material resources were more liberally available. It was a full and bustling trading place and in contrast to the impoverishment of some, there was the wealth of others. Another feature made it a prominent stage for the department store experiment— some would say for the most meaningful aspects of that experiment—and this was the extraordinarily compact nature of Liverpool. It is a city bound into the angle formed by the Mersey and its estuary, and from its maritime hub Liverpool has developed by a series of pulsations of a roughly semicircular shape. Fenced in by sea and river, these curved bands of development—commercial, working-class, suburban—have necessarily remained close-knit and concise. Where most urban centres have grown unevenly in concentric patterns, Liverpool's principle development was in one arc of the circle, which had the effect of ensuring a high density of population in proximity to and mainly orientated to the town centre. Today 40 per cent of Liverpool's retail trade is negotiated in the city centre, and that is the highest figure of any British city.

For this reason the department store had a sound chance of success in Liverpool. Velocity of turnover was essential and Liverpool could provide the necessary clientèle from its closely packed concourse of inhabitants. Liverpool became noted for a number of homegrown department stores, of which Owen Owen's and Lewis's still remain two of the most noteworthy. The small-time shopkeeper is often heard to complain of the ferocious competition of the large emporium or store, but for every Marks and Spencer there is a penny stall in a Yorkshire market or its equivalent. Mighty oaks from tiny acorns grow and it is too easily forgotten, as one becomes over familiar with brand-names, that there actually was a Woolworth or a Harrod who started and struggled from scratch.

David Lewis and Owen Owen were two such men who built from minute foundations the trading empires of today. It seems to be a guiding rule of business history that every success is highly individualised and formulas cannot be slavishly repeated with much hope of a second triumph. Certainly Lewis and Owen were different in background and approach. Lewis came from a successful Jewish merchant family, and he established a retail concern not unlike several other such enterprises both in England

and the USA which have been associated with Jewish business interest. Owen Owen came from Welsh Wesleyan stock, with a mixed background of farming and drapery, far removed from the sophisticated manners of London merchant society in which David Lewis had been bred. However, Nonconformity has been as fruitful as Jewry in providing England with service industries, as the Cadburys and Rowntrees exemplify. Here, indirectly, was a similarity. Both the Hebraic and Wesleyan faiths seem to instil into their receptive sons the businesslike virtues of conscientiousness, indefatigable zeal, attention to detail, and a careful sense of financial husbandry. All these admirable virtues Owen Owen and David Lewis shared in abundance.

David Lewis was a good twenty years the older. He was born in 1824, the son of Wolfe Levy, a London merchant. As a youngster of fifteen he came to Liverpool in 1839 to serve a gentlemanly kind of apprenticeship with Hyam's of Lord Street. This was not a merchant house, like his father's or like one or two others in Liverpool which were patronised solely by the gentry and indulged neither in advertising nor shop frontage, and merely acted as genteel agents for the well-to-do. On the contrary, Hyam was in the garment trade at all levels, and David Lewis learnt most of what there was to know about clothing all sectors of the public. Most working-class clothes were sold by peddlers and Lewis mastered this aspect of the trade. He also came to know the new Liverpool market hall (built in 1822) intimately and he travelled widely as well, becoming especially well-connected in Manchester, where he was later to develop his business.

Owen Owen was born near Machynlleth in 1848. He studied the subtle arts of salesmanship, not in Liverpool, but in Bath. From an early age he lived there with his uncle Samuel, in whose drapers' shop he gained the most rewarding first-hand experience. Like Lewis his apprenticeship was in clothing—a considerable number of departmental stores have been founded on clothes and their accessories. The central focus of such stores may be recalled; these were places to visit to make occasional purchases, such as suits or hats, where centralised location and latitude of choice were essential. The chain stores and supermarkets of a later era were to concentrate on foodstuffs and groceries, which needed a much more localised and day-by-day incidence.

The disparity in their ages was foreshortened substantially

when it came to striking out alone. Owen Owen came to Liverpool in 1868 as a somewhat solemn twenty-year-old and within weeks established his own business, only a dozen years after David Lewis had decided to go it alone. In 1856, then aged thirty-two, he had commenced business in his own right, having had the considerable advantage of seventeen years' experience in and around Merseyside.

Lewis obtained his first premises at 44 Ranelagh Street. It was not quite in the fashionable mercantile area and, when it came to extension, he was to have a struggle with a former employee, Jacobs, who had a business at 40 Ranelagh Street. Eventually heated argument gave way to sensible compromise and soon Lewis obtained the use of five other shops on either side of No 44. Owen Owen's business origins were even less propitious. With but small capital, he had to settle for premises in London Road among some unsalubrious houses and shops. At the same time the cheapness of the property made it simpler for him to expand, and by 1873 he had over 1,000 square yards of shop floor-space.

Lewis began by selling men's and boys' suits, in particular the then fashionable knickerbocker suit, and he concentrated on properly fitting suits in an age when only the rich had been able to afford tailoring. Owen's small capital prevented him from being quite so ambitious. He started with accessories and fancy goods, selling items like ties, belts, crinolines, and gloves. The popular impression of the successful businessman is of the gambler, the man willing to take hair-raising risks upon which fortunes might be won or lost, but neither Owen nor Lewis were of that mould. They were both dedicated and singleminded businessmen whose genius lay in taking pains: they were both intent on high turnover and a low profit margin, but this principle they approached with an almost frightening caution. David Lewis was especially careful to abide by the 'cash only' financial rule, breaking with the idea of credit either to wholesaler or customer which, while it gave rise to difficulties in stock-building, meant that his solvency was never threatened. One of the twenty-year-old Owen's rules 'to guide me', as he wrote on his arrival in Liverpool 'to the Harbour of Best Success', was to 'pay debts as soon as possible so as to owe no man; and give no credit to anyone for longer period than two months; this can't be thought of at first'.

At a time when much retailing meant haggling at market stalls and with pedlars, Lewis and later Owen insisted on one price and no arguments. It was a low price and a bargain price. Added to that, every care was taken to ensure satisfaction. Lewis had a 'satisfaction guaranteed' rule to which he adhered rigidly, and both attended to the minutest detail of their shops with a military precision. Even in his later years David Lewis was normally in his store awaiting the arrival of his staff, while Owen Owen became legendary for his early morning inspections of all facets of his business, placing an incomparable accent on personal service whatever the style of purchase or purchaser. Courteous and impeccable floorwalkers, a full platoon of pageboys, special messengers and home fittings were all part of a scrupulously civil and elaborate service.

Owen could not at first afford to advertise. He concentrated on immaculate service and the kind of picturesque window-dressing which was still a novelty in the 1870s. David Lewis, on the other hand, was an extrovert and insouciant advertiser, one of the very first of that band maligned then as now for vulgarity and deception. His advertising was in fact chaste by modern standards and tastefully colourful by Victorian standards. His campaign to sell Lewis's 'two shilling tea' was pleasing, wholehearted and reputable, and another popular device was the sale of halfpenny memorandum books, replete with information about Lewis's goods and of a more general nature. Lewis's penny readings were also highly popular. These were moral or literary writings and reprints, one of the first of which related Lewis's own life and work. Such well-meaning ventures as penny readings and memorandum books were commercially successful and, although some competitors spoke of vulgarisation, they appealed to Victorian instincts of earnestness and self-help. David Lewis's last advertising fling was planned by him, but postdated his death by three months. As part of the Liverpool International Exhibition of 1886 a famous ship of the day, *The Great Eastern*, was purchased, converted and anchored in the Mersey Estuary. It proved a tremendous success and acted as a fitting obituary to a master of commercial exhibitionism. Over half a million people visited the exciting delights of *The Great Eastern* and that celebrated showman, Barnum, expressed an envious admiration. It was the nearest thing ever to a Mersey equivalent of a Mississippi showboat.

An early prosperity was the reward for the flair and diligence of the two storekeepers. In 1864 Lewis added women's clothes to his stocks and in 1874 women's shoes; tea became another speciality and in 1879, rather unusually, Lewis floated a wide-ranging tobacco department and, a little later, he embarked on an equally broad run of patent medicines. More and more attention was paid to the female shopper, particularly as the benefits of industrialism were now permeating much lower in the social hierarchy. Money was now a little freer and more people were able to afford little luxuries. Moreover, the number of items regarded as necessities and not extravagances was growing—a sure sign of rising standards and a challenge to the retail trade. The swing from manufacture on the premises to outside bulk purchasing was also very evident; in 1886, for example, Lewis's had on offer a quarter of a million hats at 3s 11d each.

For his part, Owen Owen persisted with clothing and draperies, but the very scale and scope of his enterprise made it one of the north's largest stores by the turn of the century. Variety and quality, coupled with cheapness, was the attraction for thousands on Merseyside. Dress and curtain materials were probably becoming the centrepiece of Owen's business and he was one of the first storekeepers to organise sales both shrewdly and frequently. From the onset his emphasis was on the feminine side, whereas Lewis always catered rather more for masculine custom. Considerable activity continued behind the scenes, with dozens of girls busily sewing, altering, cleaning, button-making, and the like, and it cast something of a social cachet on the apprentice or shop-assistant lucky enough to be employed at either store where, in spite of strict discipline, conditions were relatively pleasant and a filial, if patronising, atmosphere prevailed.

Where the two substantially differed was in their attitude to outward expansion. By the seventies some concerns, notably in the bakery or grocery line, were developing chains of stores, and David Lewis decided to emulate them by innovating a string of departmental stores. In 1877 his Manchester store was opened in Market Street and, as an enterprise programmed on his Liverpool experience, it was destined for a profitable future in a city he knew well. His Liverpool store had been of necessity developed in piecemeal fashion, but now in Manchester it was possible to adjust departmentalism to architecture and each floor concentrated on one or two appropriate specialities, with the sturdy stand-by of tailoring still maintained on the top storey. Later on, branches were opened in Birmingham and, not too happily, in Sheffield.

Before this empire-building outside Liverpool, Lewis had attempted expansion nearer home. As early as 1859 he had opened premises in the more fashionable Bold Street quarter, but this had not proved too profitable a move. The Lewis technique in Bold Street fell perhaps between the two stools of popular location and fashionable merchant-house. Lewis plumped for the latter. In 1878 he opened a Bon Marché store in Basnett Street and even used the Parisian colour-scheme on his vans and advertising. He retained the principle of rapid turnover and marginal profit but used it as a weapon to attack the seats of high fashion. The new store was next to Lee's—George Henry Lee was yet another of Liverpool's pioneer retail revolutionaries—and the enterprise was backed by heavy prestige advertising campaigns. The departments were dramatically frenchified, particularly when one considers the insularity of the age. Perfumes, layettes, cosmetics, toilet articles and rather daring excursions into ladies' fashions formed the pattern of Bon Marché.

France, Paris, and Boucicaut's Bon Marché had an intense fascination for England's large-scale shopkeepers and the tradition of design and taste they transferred to their own enterprises was to add considerably to the style of English retailing. Owen Owen sent buyers to the Parisian fashion salons, and the modes they brought home to Liverpool excited a good deal of commercial interest. Owen Owen also invested, merely as a sleeping partner, in the Bon Marché shop in Brixton. His investments were in fact varied and extensive as he bought heavily in the real estate and in other markets distinct from retailing, and at the time of his death he had amassed quite a fortune.

It is strange that he was relatively content with the single success of Audley House, as Owen Owen's headquarters came to be known. David Lewis followed the more natural line of trading colonialism, but Owen preferred to use the profits from his one store for wide-ranging entrepreneurship. It may have been linked with family interests. Both men married fairly late in life. Lewis married Bertha Cohen in 1859 when he was thirty-five. His wife, well connected in both Jewish cultural and commercial circles, proved a stalwart prop in business and a charming hostess in society. On his marriage Lewis moved from his home in Clarence Street to Faulkner Square and then, in 1864, to Prince's Park, where he lived until his death, scarcely more than a brisk walk from the business. Although the couple had no children, members of the family were encouraged to join the firm. A chief example of this policy was Louis Cohen, who was to become David Lewis's main successor. He was a nephew of Bertha Lewis and he completed the family grouping tidily by marrying David's niece, May Levy. This sustained filial interest must have encouraged David Lewis to extend his business to accommodate other talented members of his family.

It was rather different with Owen Owen, who was even later in sampling the joys of matrimony. At forty-four, he married a southern lady called Ellen Richards in 1891 and soon left Merseyside to settle in London, where he had plenty of property interests. He maintained his authoritarian command of the store, but he was not over-anxious to involve his four children, preferring to see them as professional men capable of organising his broadly based fiscal interests, rather than as commercial men. This line of thought doubtless confirmed his policy of non-expansion.

The factor of family was to affect the progress of both stores seriously. Neither man lived to a ripe old age; indeed, each died in his early sixties. David Lewis was sixty-one when he died on 5 December 1885 after a long illness. 'Latterly it has been felt', said the *Liverpool Daily Albion* dolefully, 'that his case was hopeless.' Two days later he was buried at the Hebrew Cemetery, Fairfield. It was a plain but 'imposing' funeral accompanied by twenty broughams. As it progressed through Liverpool the crowds of women forced past the police in an 'inconvenient manner' and there was some confusion before what the *Courier* called 'decorous order' was restored. The tight mesh of family control and their experience of his commercial ventures left the lifework of David Lewis in secure hands. There was a critical setback exactly a year later when the Liverpool store was gutted by fire on Christmas Eve, but Louis Cohen and his fellow directors were advancing confidently into the future. When David Lewis died, his department store was the largest in Liverpool.

Owen Owen died suddenly in the spring of 1910, aged sixty-two. He failed to survive a minor operation and the abruptness of his death came as a shock both personally and commercially.

The retail revolution: David Lewis and Owen Owen

Owen Owen's children were too young to assume control, whereas David Lewis's family had been interwoven into the business skilfully and the very length of his final illness had given a useful, if unhappy, period for readjustment. There was no firm nor inspired hand to replace Owen Owen's. In spite of living in the south, his careful supervision of the firm had not wavered and this very autocratic control now militated against the business when its founder died. After a few years of somewhat false prosperity, partly connected with the unreal economic situation of the First World War, Owen Owen's slumped badly in the 1920s and struggled desperately to overcome a series of severe crises. Eventually the business recovered. In 1925 the present Owen Owen's building was opened in Clayton Square where, after an uneasy start, it settled down to a bracing commercial tempo, concentrating on a rather more select and fashionable market. The important corollary to this was the deal negotiated in 1927 with yet another renowned Liverpool shopkeeper, T. J. Hughes. He transferred his business to Audley House and soon built up a powerful enterprise, dwelling on somewhat more popular lines than the Clayton Square store. Duncan Norman, husband of Owen Owen's daughter Dilys, and T. J. Hughes together formulated a rare and invigorating partnership, one which has served as the foundation for a constantly prospering and expanding retail business.

Both firms have stood the test of time, the one firm smoothly, the other after some domestic difficulties. They are among the largest of Liverpool department stores and their links extend throughout and beyond Great Britain. Like those most celebrated of shopkeepers, Marks and Spencer, Owen and Lewis were socially conscious in some degree. It was revealed in 1892 that the residue of the Lewis estate, amounting eventually to some £350,000, had been left to Benjamin Levy, David Lewis's nephew, and to Benjamin's brother-in-law, George Cohen. It was to be held in trust and invested for the benefit of the Manchester and Liverpool poor. The Liverpool press was fruitful in its gratuitous advice on how the money should be spent; pension schemes, housing associations, women's welfare homes, and almshouses were canvassed possibilities. The David Lewis hotel, restaurant, and theatre in Liverpool 8 form the major testimony to the generosity of David Lewis, while Owen Owen demonstrated his social commitment during his lifetime with an emergency trust fund for employees, staff hostels, a sports ground and a number of other pleasing gestures. He was one of the first major storekeepers to introduce the weekly halfday holiday for his employees. Both had proved to be benevolent despots.

Apart from their social consciences and the application of a revolutionary retail technique, they must also be remembered for a meaningful feature which perhaps coalesced these social and economic elements. The centenary history of Lewis's, and Owen Owen's fine centenary commemoration book, have respectively the company slogans *Friends of the People* and *They Always Come Back* as their titles. These mottoes point up the socio-economic restructuring of the successful department store. On the one hand, they enforced high standards of integrity and fair dealing. When both men began work, standards were often shoddy and deceitful, a fact that was most vividly evident in foodstuffs, where milk was sophisticated, cheese harmfully coloured, butter watered, and condiments enlivened with such substances as brickdust and sulphuric acid. One of the chief motivating forces of the co-operative movement was the avoidance of adulteration and it was only in the last quarter of the century that official steps against reprehensible trading practices were enforced with any effect. Both Owen and Lewis insisted on commercial justice for the customer and, needless to say, it paid them handsome dividends. They were unavowedly competitive, but it was their boast that they sided with the shopper against the common antagonist of the high-price storekeeper and middleman. One or two half-hearted attempts to impose trading boycotts came to nothing because the Owen Owen and Lewis outlets were so flowing. They cut prices and avoided middlemen. In the 1880s the Lewis organisation advertised that 'this is a very good thing for the public, but not so pleasant for the middleman'. The insistence of these retail princes on a fair deal did much to run the devious Victorian traders out of business.

On the other hand, there was a democratising proclivity about both stores which is as important to the social remoulding of shopping as high commercial standards. The long working day, with stores perhaps open twelve hours, helped a little in this respect, for the more peaceful spacing of custom assisted in evoking a calm and dignified atmosphere. Into this attractive and sedate world of a million commodities, every customer, however low his social rank or trivial his need, was welcomed with an all but ostentatious civility. Owen Owen and Lewis's were soon noted for the classless nature of their clientèle, from the tradesmen's wife seeking out a bargain to the merchant's lady arriving in carriage with manservant in tow. It can be argued that the classless nature of consumption, pioneered by men like Owen and Lewis, is more realistic an aspect of egalitarianism than any political or economic device. Around the 1870s, David Lewis made the point admirably in one of his many advertisements in which he referred modestly to the patronage of the Queen and the Earl of Derby and other notable figures. But, he continued, the owners 'pride themselves upon the fact that their business is essentially with the masses'.

It was a long haul. It is difficult to gauge exactly how the two were regarded outside their personal and business circles at that time. The one a Jew and the other in later life a Unitarian—both were by nature and profession a trifle off the normal beam. The obituaries on David Lewis in the Liverpool press are strangely muted. They are brief and they damn with faint praise, especially compared with the eulogistic paeans which followed local politicoes and celebrities to their final resting places. The *Daily Albion* described him as 'a persistent, consistent advertiser' and that was about the nearest to praise Liverpool's largest store-owner received until the news of his bequest drew belated plaudits from the newspapers.

It must be granted that Lewis and Owen floated the right businesses at the right time. Liverpool, in the 1850s, was handling a huge fraction of British trade while the last half of the last century showed a widening chasm between rising wages and declining prices unknown either before or since. It was, of course, a propitious time for others to seize that opportunity. David Lewis and Owen Owen were two of the very few who did so with consummate success and few historical characters can boast such lively and money-spinning monuments as the Londoner and the Welshman who came to Liverpool to open shops.

CHAPTER TEN

The fame of Florence Maybrick

Cities tend to have one or more folk-villains associated with them, murderers who excite the passionate interest of the public to the point where they pass into the grimmer galleries of folk-lore. Edinburgh has Burke and Hare; Chicago has Leopold and Loeb, the 'superman' murders; Manchester has Charlie Peace and the dreadful Moors Murderers; London has a gruesome collection including Jack the Ripper, Hawley Crippen, and Christie. Given its rumbustious and often brutal past, Liverpool has an oddly delicate record in such matters. Most of its well-known murderers have been mysterious rather than violent. After the Maybrick case, probably Liverpool's most notable mystery has been the killing of Julia Wallace in 1931, of which it has been written that 'the Wallace Case is more than a classic, it is *the* classic of criminology'. Briefly, her husband was charged with the murder, convicted and, in a unique decision released by the Appeal Court on the unprecedented ground that the jury's verdict 'cannot be supported having regard to the evidence'. Wallace either created an alibi by sending a fake telephone message to himself to visit an insurance client called 'Qualtrough', or 'Qualtrough' tricked him into leaving his wife alone, murdered her and left the husband heavily incriminated. It is that rare case where one set of accepted circumstances perfectly fits two directly opposed hypotheses, and as such it has given rise to long, profound academic debate.

Forty-two years earlier Florence Maybrick had initiated a similar series of criminological discussions, although in her case they have been more popular and excitable and less scholastic and dispassionate. It is reminiscent of the journalists' convention which invented the best-selling headline including race, vice, homicide, religion, and sex: 'Negro Dope-addict Slays Lay-Preacher's Mistress'. The Maybrick case had everything; it appears to have comprehended every last cliché of the most melodramatic novelette. Florence Elizabeth Chandler, born in Mobile in 1862, was a Southern belle, left a little short of prettiness by an overfull upper lip, but pert and lively and personable. In 1881, aged eighteen, she married James Maybrick, a Liverpool cotton-broker, twenty-three years her senior. A hard-living man, he kept a salesgirl sporadically over twenty years and fathered five children by her. For her part Florence had at least one extra-marital encounter with one Alfred Brierley, and this played a meaningful part in deciding her fate.

At a time when the marriage was under some strain—there was an angry scene at the Grand National in March—Maybrick, a notorious hypochondriac, fell ill toward the end of April 1889. After a brief respite, he grew worse. In suspicious circumstances and with Florence forbidden by his family from attending the invalid, he died on the evening of 10 May. Mrs Maybrick was convicted of poisoning him after a week's trial, but substantial opinion on both sides of the Atlantic rallied to her side. Literally, she was snatched from the foot of the gallows; three days before the intended execution at Walton Prison the sentence was commuted to life imprisonment, and after fifteen years' imprisonment, singularly unpleasant for one used to a cosy middle-class life, she was released. She lived out a remarkably long if predictably vacillating life in the States, dying, aged seventy-nine, in 1941. She was an old recluse, all but destitute, and more than a trifle eccentric.

So much for the bare outline. The dramatic overtones were shattering. There was the marriage of cotton, Florence from its source and James from its point of marketing. There was the international flavour. Not only was there the Anglo-American détente, with the rumblings of the campaign touching the British embassy and even the White House, there was the spice added by Florence's mother. A Northerner, she had married a highly eligible Southerner, William Chandler, and then, six months after his death, she married Captain du Barry, a courageous officer of the Confederate army. He, too, died within months. Both died of doubtful causes and in a mysterious fashion during the fervour of the American Civil War, and rumour was on both occasions rife that she had poisoned the pair of them. Her third marriage, a violent and ill-omened affair with a Prussian cavalryman, Baron von Roques, only added a continental piquancy to the image. Poison continued to run in the family. Florie Maybrick's son James died in 1911, having drunk from a beaker of potassium cyanide. The coroner's jury returned a verdict, somewhat surprisingly, of accidental death. Mrs Maybrick's other child, Gladys, married a naval officer and led a more prosaic but also more pleasant existence than the rest of her family.

Apart from the poison and the international overtones, there was the clash of May and December in the Maybrick household. It has been suggested that, in legendary Victorian fashion, Maybrick had dreamed up hopes of financial support through his marriage, hopes stimulated by the hyperbolic narrative not so much of Florence but of her tempestuous mother. If it was not quite a case of 'her beauty was sold for an old man's gold', it was certainly made clear that 'youth cannot match with age'. The wide gap in their ages contributed to the difficulties of the marriage and the serious decline in Maybrick's business—he had an office in Tithebarn Street—scarcely helped. She was, of course, in alien climes, and despite a certain social success, she seems to have lacked intimate friends and advisers. The Maybrick family were mostly cool towards her and regarded her mother and herself as opportunists. The effective head of the family was James' brother, Michael, who oddly enough had turned away from textiles to music, but he was no aesthetic young Jolyon. More of a musical Soames, he was the most successful of the family and he is best known for his compositions, *The Holy City* and *Star of Bethlehem*.

Towards the end of James Maybrick's life, suspicions were aroused to the extent that Michael Maybrick made Florence virtually a prisoner in her own home and thus left it to posterity to accept that she still continued her murderous ways and outwitted both family and servants. It would seem to have been foolish to sustain the murder attempt after discovery and yet extremely clever to have completed it. The nursemaid, the aptly named Alice Yapp, opened a letter to Florie's lover and Michael Maybrick was informed of the contents. She weakly claimed she opened the letter after it had dropped in some mud as she took it to the post. Two family friends, Mrs Briggs and Mrs Hughes, also appear in bad light, for they seemed to have raised suspicions against Mrs Maybrick whilst pretending friendship. On the same day that Edwin Maybrick, having been shown the incriminating letter by the inquisitive Miss Yapp, telegraphed his brother Michael, Mrs Briggs also sent him a telegram reading: 'Come at once strange things going on here.' Two such telegrams in the space of a day brought Michael scurrying to Liverpool. They isolated Florence and, following her husband's death, they searched the house and found several caches of arsenic. All kinds of evidence about Florence tampering with medicines and meat-juices was later forthcoming.

Rarely, then, has a convicted murderess been so closely watched and so firmly suspected before the fell deed. Her position was one of such alienation that some commentators have argued that the Maybrick brothers, Mrs Brigg and Mrs Hughes and the nurse-maid Alice Yapp formed a formidable conspiracy against Florence Maybrick, an argument that has even been extended to the extreme of hinting that this cabal was, in fact, responsible for Maybrick's death.

Alfred Brierley should have received the letter intercepted by Alice Yapp. Her flirtatious temperament and the frigidity of the family circle drove Florence Maybrick probably into a series of dalliances, of which the brief affair with young Brierley was the last and fatal one. Throughout the trial he trembled at the back of the court but was not called. It has been said that the May-bricks were not anxious to wash dirty linen in public, particularly as many thought a piece or so of the laundry attached to Edwin Maybrick. Brierley left Liverpool immediately after the trial to start a fresh life. Alternately, the Maybricks were relieved that, apparently on Florence's instructions, the defence resisted the temptation to blazon James Maybrick's transgressions before the jury.

A wife with a lover and a husband with a mistress—yet another dimension of the newsworthiness of the case. The opposed responses are fascinatingly Victorian. The twenty years or more of James Maybrick's cavorting and his five illegitimate children were easily glossed over. It was even regarded as manly and hearty. It is arguable that Florence's weekend with Brierley, her only known extra-marital encounter, convicted her. In his sum-ming-up Judge Stephen changed overnight. He was firstly leniently disposed toward the prisoner, but on the last day of the trial he launched a vehement attack on her, giving vent to 'a horrible and incredible thought that a woman should be plotting the death of her husband in order that she might be at liberty to follow her own degrading vices . . . it is easy enough to conceive how a horrible woman in so terrible a position might be assailed by some fearful and terrible temptation'. It has been said that Mr Justice Stephen, certain that the evidence was too flimsy for a conviction, was determined to hand out a verbal flailing as punishment for Mrs Maybrick's immorality.

If that stolen weekend convicted Florie Maybrick, it also ensured her a long imprisonment. In spite of the most frenzied campaigns, with many notable persons involved, not the least Sir Charles Russell, her defence counsel, who never ceased to struggle for her release, she lay jailed year after year. Her energetic mother, the woman's suffrage movement, a phalanx of writers, lawyers, diplomats, and friends; no one could persuade the government to budge out of either justice or mercy. It was Queen Victoria herself, a symbol of womanly purity, who was the obstacle. She accepted Mrs Maybrick's salvation from the gallows with ill grace, writing that 'the only regret she feels is that so wicked a woman should escape by a mere legal quibble . . . but her sentence must never be further commuted'. Successive Home Secretaries felt unable, whatever their constitutional position, to tangle with that formidable monarch on a question of feminine concern. Very obviously, Queen Victoria's death led with almost indecent haste to an announcement that Mrs Maybrick would be paroled (not pardoned) in three years' time. Some of this parole was spent at an Anglican retreat in Cornwall, an arrangement made by the Duchess of Bedford which was a considerate act aimed at preparing Mrs Maybrick for a world strange and changed by 1904 from the one she knew in 1889.

It was this constant bombardment upon the government that succeeded in keeping the case in the public eye. Hardly a year passed without the whole sorry business being rehearsed and rehashed. Everything was tried, from spiritualist interventions and deathbed confessions in the heart of Africa to a letter, penned in his own hand, from President McKinley to Queen Victoria on the occasion of her diamond jubilee. After her release and contrary to the terms of her ticket-of-leave, Mrs Maybrick wrote a flowery book describing her experiences and demonstrating, as always, her characteristic propensity for exaggeration and even untruth; she stumped the States on a lecture-tour delineating prison conditions; she was up to the ears in all kinds of property transactions and related legal affairs; there was once or twice a hint of new romance. From about the end of the First World War she dropped into obscurity, but the death of an enfeebled, decayed old woman in October 1941 set the name of Maybrick shouting from the headlines again. From the trial onwards and right up until the present time, a torrent of commentaries have kept this most open issue alive. At a conservative estimate eight books have been devoted solely to her case, and dozens more include a section or chapter on the mystery. Half a dozen novels have been inspired by the case.

The notoriety of the Maybrick case was afforded a tremendous impetus by the trial itself. It was conducted at St George's Hall through a warm summer week and with public attention taut and massive. There was the clash of Addison and Russell, the former a competent, dispassionate lawyer, the latter better known and more histrionic. There were bitter academic contests of a complicated nature concerning arsenic, its degree of fatality and its medical effects. There was Mrs Maybrick's own statement, usually regarded as a defence blunder, in which she told how her husband 'implored me then to give him this powder'. Many think this tacit admission turned the case. There was a judge of great merit and intellect, who stumbled badly during the case and ended it with that thundering denunciation of poor Florie's morals. He soon after resigned the bench because of ill health and ended his days in an Ipswich lunatic asylum, a progression never forgotten by Mrs Maybrick's assorted champions. There was the jury of stolid tradesmen, with Thomas Wainwright, a Southport plumber, their foreman. They found the accused guilty in thirty-eight minutes flat, foreshadowing the equally speedy conviction of Wallace forty years on. The jury's hasty conclusion, given the perplexing character of the evidence, is an unpleasant aspect of the case. Feminists attributed it to the jurors deciding 'for their sex'. There was also an outcry on the lax procedures for managing the jury, who had wined and dined at a nearby hotel, discussing the case openly with the clientèle.

It has frequently been stated that, irrespective of Florence's guilt or otherwise, she should not have been convicted in law on the trial evidence. Because of this, her case was further focused on public attention by its deployment in the struggle for an appeal court which eventually was established in 1907. Lawyers have argued interminably about the case, and it even managed to get itself enmeshed, by Sir Charles Russell's politics, in the Irish Question. That it was a most confused affair is patently evident from the decision not to hang the prisoner. After all kinds of consultation, legal, medical, and political, part of the text of the commutation order read: 'Although the evidence leads clearly to the conclusion that the prisoner administered and attempted to administer arsenic to her husband with intent to murder, yet it does not wholly exclude a reasonable doubt whether his death was in fact caused by the administration of arsenic.' In other words, Mrs Maybrick was sentenced to life imprisonment for a crime—attempted murder—for which she had neither been charged nor tried. As *The Times* remarked, 'it makes things comfortable all round for the experts'.

The Times' sympathetic interest illustrated the vast following the case created. Populace and press eagerly hung on every word and move, and few were neutral. Most people and journals took up a position as if it were a race or a football match. 'It was the biggest thing of our day,' said a reporter. Many were pleased to observe their betters being brought to book, just as others argued that only Mrs Maybrick's social standing and American nationality saved her from death at the hands of Berry, most phlegmatic of hangmen. There were hisses, swoonings and shoutings in court when the verdict was announced. The judge was mobbed when he left St George's Hall and the convicted murderess was applauded. Later there was a counter-demonstration, and soon after the trial, meetings for and against were being fully attended not only in Liverpool but throughout the land. Petitions signed by half a million people flooded into the Home Office from over two hundred towns. Seventy thousand Liverpolitans signed the mercy plea, together with a thousand members of the Liverpool Exchange, of which James Maybrick had been a member. As often happens, there was a revulsion of feeling after the conviction. 'The friendless lady' was suddenly befriended on all sides. The wily broadsheet hawkers of Liverpool began to push the legend with verses for on one side and verses against on the other of their broadsides. At a slightly higher level of entertainment, Tussaud's displayed a Maybrick wax effigy in splendid isolation and the Sadler's Wells Theatre hurriedly produced a melodrama entitled *The Poisoner*.

Thus from the beginning the case enjoyed a full-throated emotional appeal scarcely paralleled in criminal history. The infamous rogues of Tussaud's chamber of horrors excite mainly dislike and disgust. Mrs Maybrick attracted both affectionate sympathy (including several proposals of marriage just after her trial) and venomous ire. And, as with Wallace and a few other cases, the major question still remained for unending debate as to whether or not she was guilty. It is perhaps conceivable that had Florence Maybrick been hanged, the argument might have been buried with her. The question of her treatment and release conjoined with the issue of her innocence to sustain popular and academic interest. Mrs Maybrick even tried malingering, endeavouring to simulate a lung affliction by self-mutilation. Her health in prison became yet another talking-point and opportunity to revise the case yet once more. All the while new 'evidence' was being made available or the authorities were being accused of withholding it. Maybrickiana became a small industry.

The use of poison was as typical of the nineteenth century as the lurid public reaction to the tale of a poisoned husband. Renaissance Italy apart, it is difficult to think of an age more dedicated to poison than the Victorian. There has scarcely been a noted twentieth-century poisoner. The contemporary murderers who have won themselves a high place in popular annals have, perhaps typically of the epoch, usually been the perpetrators of violent, sexually perverse crimes; one thinks of Christie, Hanratty, Haigh, Heath, Brady and Hindley. Even Crippen, convicted in 1910, is rightly associated with that previous era of poisoners. Poison was reasonably available and drugs were being used increasingly, but toxicology was in its infancy, and the chances of discovery were less than nowadays when pathological techniques are so sophisticated.

Poisoning is sometimes thought of as a feminine tactic because it is independent of actual physical strength. Nevertheless the Victorian and Edwardian era boasted any number of male poisoners, and some of the more infamous names include Billy Palmer, 'the Rugeley Poisoner'; George Chapman, who poisoned at least three women; Neill Cream, the strychnine poisoner; Wainewright, 'the literary poisoner' and friend of Wordsworth; and the miserly Frederick Seddon. Not that the distaff side were laggards. Mary Ann Burdock was executed in 1835 at Bristol for arsenical poisoning, and Sarah Chesham was hanged at Chelmsford for the same offence in 1851. Catharine Wilson, a wholesale arsenical poisoner, was hanged at Newgate in 1862.

Two cases prior to Mrs Maybrick's were especially interesting. One was the celebrated affair of Madeline Smith, accused of murdering her lowborn lover to embark on a high-class Glasgow marriage. The death by arsenic of L'Angelier, her foreign-born sweetheart, had sensational consequences in the staid Glasgow social circles of 1857. She obtained a 'Not Proven' verdict which has been ironically paraphrased as 'not guilty, but don't do it again'. The case has been the subject of books, plays, and films, and some features of it make it uncommonly like the Maybrick story—one might assume that Mrs Maybrick was aware of the tale of the handsome, composed Miss Smith. Nearer home and later in time was the case, in 1884, of two Liverpool sisters, Mrs Flanagan and Mrs Higgins, who fed arsenic to three relatives and a lodger to collect their life insurances. They were hanged at Kirkdale Prison. All Liverpool, and not least Mrs Maybrick, must have known of this local and recent poisoning. All three cases, interestingly enough, involved the extraction of arsenic from fly-papers. Whether one conceives of Mrs Maybrick picking up tips from this inglorious tradition or whether one imagines its effect on the public mentality, it is certain that the factor of poison was yet another element in the growth of the Maybrick legend. The very cunning and unscrupulous intrigue of the poisoner, essentially a long-term planner of the death of an intimate friend or relation, ensures him or her a reluctantly fascinated audience.

It is arsenic which ultimately makes the Maybrick case so astounding. There is little doubt that the appropriately if oddly named Battlecrease House was full of drugs, including relatively large quantities of arsenic. The Maybrick's large rented house at Aigburth, overlooking the Liverpool cricket club, of which James was a member, contained scores of bottles of medicines and nostrums of all kinds. The use of arsenic by both husband and wife reflects some of the bizarre quirks of the Victorian well-to-do strata. While it is evident that Florence Maybrick, like Madeline Smith, used arsenic in cosmetic preparations, it is equally assured that her husband used arsenic, with a countless series of other frightening concoctions, including strychnine and prussic acid, for his health. He attempted to restore his general well-being and sexual vigour by imbibing arsenic and other drugs, so much so that one theory suggests that he died of abstinence and withdrawal symptoms when the poisons were no longer administered.

Both Maybrick and his wife were not unduly anxious to disclose their indulgence in arsenic. James Maybrick was not keen to broadcast his drug-taking around Merseyside society, while Florence Maybrick was modestly reticent about her cosmetic devices, preferring to buy fly-papers or poison for rats. Fly-papers were soaked to prepare the necessary face-wash. These small pretences or subterfuges were typical of the minor hypocrisies of the age. It is, to the modern mind, incredible that a married couple could both have indulged in arsenic, largely in ignorance of one another's practices.

Add to this the exceedingly wide guesses of conflicting experts on the measure of a fatal dose and their controversial accounts of the irritant symptoms of arsenic, and the case grows yet more in complexity. Florence had an excuse for having arsenic in Battlecrease House, but was this an ingenious cover, perhaps culled from previous cases, for an unpleasant murder, or did it merely make it simpler for her accusers to point the condemning finger? James had a reason, however misguided, for taking arsenic, but did this make it that much easier to cast the blame on his wife, or did it simplify Florence's homicidal activities? Some commentators have stated that it would be impossible to poison an arsenic addict with arsenic. Conversely, his very addiction might have eased the task of administering an overdose. As Lord Birkenhead put it, was Mrs Maybrick 'the tender nurse' or 'the calculating assassin'? The balance of the question is appalling. It is either black or white. If innocent, Florence Maybrick was subjected to degrading and bestial suffering, a widow, cut off from her relations and society and completely alienated from her children, neither of whom she ever again saw after her arrest. If guilty, she was as blackhearted and unpleasant a rogue as Mesdames Flanagan and Higgins. The yawning chasm between guilt and innocence in murder attracts constant reappraisal; it is not just the academic quality of the mystery, it is the polarisation of the emotions and conditions of mind involved. It must be admitted that Florence Maybrick's very conviction caused an immediate reaction in her favour, a reaction set in train partly by the revulsion against the two-faced Mrs Hughes and Alice Yapp. Possibly had Mrs Maybrick been acquitted and released, the tide would have turned the other way. It is the way of the criminological world that convictions lead to renewed efforts to prove the verdict false. In their differing ways, the cases of Timothy Evans, James Hanratty, or Lee Harvey Oswald have quite recently illustrated this proclivity. Acquittals are more difficult. Slander and libel laws protect acquitted persons from refreshed assaults, whereas no convicted person would mind a campaign in their defence. With Madeline Smith, many commentators have thought her guilty, and until recently experts have tended to judge William Wallace the murderer of his wife.

Florence Maybrick, guilty or innocent, survived her ordeal as L.P.29 in Woking and Aylesbury Gaols and outlived most of those who had been closely connected with the case. Although she died a senile and lonely recluse, her narrative lives on in both the academic annals and folk-memories of crime. It reads like a Wilkie Collins novel, and is at least as strange as fiction. Practically every possible facet of the human predicament, in its Victorian manifestation, is represented in the Maybrick case. Because of this patchwork pattern Mrs Maybrick has become in Liverpool as noted an historical figure as many a more dignified and worthy a personage.

CHAPTER ELEVEN

The sectarian troubles and the Police Inquiry of 1909-10

T he recent history of Ulster serves as a tragic reminder that the religious wars are not over. Thankfully, Liverpool's religious controversies have never been as violent as those of Belfast, or indeed, Glasgow. The city has, however, some notoriety as a centre of sectarian discontent. For many years the high Roman Catholic proportion of the population and the strength of the Orange Lodges made something of a nonsense of the conventional class breakdown of English party politics, and occasionally there have been rabid outbreaks of prejudice and disturbance. It is quieter now. Perhaps religion does not move blocs of people as emotively as it used to. Tolerance, it has been cynically remarked, is indifference. There are signs reminiscent of a less peaceful past. On Orange Day, when William III's victory at the Boyne is celebrated, the procession in Liverpool and during the lodges' outing in Southport is an incredible tour de force. Each lodge has its ocharina or fife band, its own William and Mary in a kind of principal girl and boy duo, its banners, its Bible and its orange-sashed support. Alternatively, when the new Metropolitan Cathedral was opened recently, the flats and houses around were comprehensively decked out in papal greenery together with score upon score of symbols and photographs.

In an age of hesitancy and diffidence in these matters, in a century akin to the eighteenth in its broad latitudes on religious questions, it is fascinating to observe faiths sustained with a nineteenth-century verve and assurance. Liverpool owes its vast Catholic citizenry to the Irish migrations, but not as completely as it is often assumed. South Lancashire Catholicism has a much older tradition dating to the time of the English Reformation when, led by several noble recusant families, like the Blundells, the country's Roman Catholics stuck grimly to their faith. There are villages on Merseyside and throughout Lancashire (such as Little Crosby, where the Blundell residence is located) where almost the entire population is Catholic. Preston and St Helen's both have probably a higher percentage of Roman Catholics than Liverpool. This is a long-standing South Lancashire tradition, and not only a phenomenon of the 1840s.

On the other hand, Liverpool has had obvious connections with Northern Ireland as well as with what is now Eire. The Orange tradition can be traced back beyond even the stirring tales of the Boyne and the Londonderry Apprentices to the days of Cromwell and Strafford. The Protestant ranks have always been wide; all brands and fashions of Protestantism have flourished even within the Church of England, and the identification of Anglicanism with the state has invoked the church in a permanent and sturdy political aspect. 'What makes Britain Great?' asks the Orange banner. 'The King and the Protestant Religion', comes the reply. Perhaps because of its Irish links and as a natural counterpoint to the strength of Catholicism, the Protestant politico-religious front has always been a solid one. Liverpool has had its more strictly Nonconformist sons, its Rathbones and its Charles Booth, and its Nonconformist institutions, like the famous Welsh Charity Schools, visited once by the Prince of Wales. The tendency, however, is to associate Lancashire Nonconformity with Manchester and sturdy towns like Warrington and Bolton. Gladstone, radical statesman and devout Anglican, is more typically Liverpolitan. A councillor, simply labelled 'Protestant', is at present a member of the city council.

Occasionally, then, a little heat is generated. The Liverpool citizenry are accomplished wall-daubers and a certain amount of encapsulated theology may be studied, as it were, murally. 'Billy is a Bastard' is probably the least unkind commentary on the House of Orange to appear on or about Orangemen's Day. To 'God Bless our Pope', the earnest Protestant finds it impossible not to add 'ye'. Granted that the modern hagiography—Tommy Smith, Alan Ball—receives somewhat more substantial support, religious awareness is, albeit crudely, signified. One is always surprised at the numbers of Liverpool parents who refer to state schools (not without some basic validity) as 'Protestant' schools. Obviously the thinking and concerned members of all churches are equally distressed by a commitment not much raised above the level of gang rivalry. The two cathedrals now face one another along the pleasantly titled Hope Street, the Anglican with its assured mock-Gothic lines and the confident hugeness, the Roman Catholic more immediately dramatic in its unconventional skyward swoop.

So essential concord exists, despite odd aberrations. Nevertheless, serious conflict has occurred within living memory. The year 1909 was such a time, when the classic symptoms of a miniature Ulster were manifest. There were rumours, misunderstandings and minor provocations; there were protests and demonstrations. There were confrontations and police action, accusations about police brutality and partisanship. These last were such that under a special statute, the Police (Liverpool Inquiry) Act, 1909, a commissioner was appointed to inquire into the conduct of the police during the disturbances and 'into the circumstances causing such disturbances'. Arthur J. Ashton was selected as the commissioner. A King's Counsel, he undertook his function with consummate zeal. The inquiry lasted twenty-five days, occupying most of February 1910, when dozens of witnesses were called and documents tabled, when well over 20,000 questions were posed, making a transcript that easily exceeds 1,000 folio pages. Ashton then worked with reasonable expedition to produce a seventy-page report for Herbert Gladstone, the Home Secretary, by the end of March. All in all, it represents one of the fullest accounts of sectarian strife in recent times.

It seems simplest to allow so compendious a document to speak for itself. It was unbendingly judicial in its approach, and there seems no reason to suspect either Ashton or the Liberal administration that dispatched him of axes to grind. A slight reservation only is necessary, the consequences of impartiality in excess, for Ashton sometimes sounds lofty to the point of social anthropology. In his objective sighting and observation of those rare specimens, the Liverpool policeman and religionist, he possibly misses some of the heart of the matter. His diplomatic reportage, his determination to remain 'our man in Liverpool', and his legalistic background possibly makes him err, if anything on the side of law and order. This is not a complaint, but a brief warning that many such reports tend, because of their provenance, to look kindly on the establishment.

Ashton began his summary with a short resumé of the background:

There are in Liverpool out of a population of about three-quarters of a million in all some 173,000 Roman Catholics and a vast number of strong Protestants and Orangemen. The disturbances dealt with in this Report took place in the poorer districts in the northern part of the city. . . . Among the Protestant places of worship is the Protestant Reformers' Church, which was founded in 1903, its pastor is Mr George Wise. From the first one part of the work of the Reformers' Church was carried on by a separate organisation called the 'George Wise Crusade'. The work of the George Wise Crusade was to conduct outdoor meetings at least once a week at a place called St. Domingo Pit in the E division. 'The Pit', as it was called throughout the Inquiry, is an open unenclosed space on the highway, where several roads meet, and adjoins an enclosed recreation ground, which is upon the site of the old St. Domingo Pit. Among the Protestants in these districts parades and processions are very customary. The Men's Bible Class of the Reformers' Church, now numbering 1,600, parade five times a year. The Orange lodges from time to time organise processions with bands of music. Between 1903 and 1909 practically no disturbances had occurred in connection with these processions.

In September, 1908, the Eucharistic Congress was held in London, and the Protestant party in Liverpool, as elsewhere, protested by meetings and petitions to the Government against any Eucharistic procession being held in connection with that Congress. No such procession was in fact held, but apparently distrust and suspicion was aroused in the minds of the Protestant party in Liverpool, and some, at any rate, thought that the Roman Catholic priests were angry because no Eucharistic procession had been allowed in London.

In the spring of 1909 the congregation of the Roman Catholic Church of the Holy Cross decided to celebrate in May the sixtieth anniversary of the foundation of the Mission. Holy Cross Church stands in Great Crosshall Street, in a very poor Roman Catholic area.

On 8 April 1909, the Diamond Jubilee Decoration Committee, formed by the Holy Cross Young Men's Society, requested the Liverpool Health Committee for permission to decorate the streets of the parish and progress through them on 9 May and 'to sanction the erection of an altar at the junction of Standish Street and Marybone (by the fountain), in commemoration of an event of historical and religious interest'. The Health Committee agreed, but by one of those bizarre quirks of municipal protocol, although theirs was the right to speak on street decoration, the city fountains fell under the odd auspices of the Finance Committee. A local Roman Catholic councillor, Mr Burke, acquainted the police with the nature of the event, but the Head Constable had no knowledge of the Health Committee correspondence.

From this seemingly innocent incident a sectarian conflict stealthily developed.

On April 30th the following letter was sent to the Chief Constable:

> 'Loyal Orange Institution of England,
> Province of Liverpool, Circuit No. 1,
> Provincial Grand Secretary's Office,
> 65, Linacre Lane, Bootle,
>
> April 30th 1909.
>
> Sir, I am given to understand that a Roman Catholic procession and carrying of the Host in the public streets is to take place in Liverpool on Sunday, the 9th prox. If the latter is permitted I venture to say that it will lead to serious trouble with the members of above organisation and other Protestant bodies, and I sincerely hope, in the common interests of peace, that wise counsel will prevail and that you will use your good offices to prevent it taking place.
>
> I am, sir,
> Yours faithfully,
> A. B. COLTER.
>
> To the Chief Constable,
> Liverpool.'

The Head Constable discussed this with Councillor Burke, and here a genuine misunderstanding arose. The Head Constable, Leonard Dunning, felt that Burke offered an assurance 'that neither the Host, nor relics, nor statues, nor anything of the kind, would be carried', whereas Burke thought he had tendered his 'own private opinion' and no pledge that this was the case. Dunning notified Colter as to this purported assurance, and he also informed the Lord Mayor that no ceremonial would be performed nor emblem carried through the streets. It should perhaps be explained that this was no mere emotional issue. The carriage of the Host, the wearing of vestments, the performance of sacramental ceremony and other religious acts in the streets were severely forbidden at this time by the Roman Catholic Emancipation Act of 1829. In effecting a frame of tolerance for Catholics, that statute had expressly drawn the line at public shows of papalism, presumably thinking that the Protestant majority might be antagonised or endangered. This legislation, reluctantly forced on Wellington and Peel by political circumstances, had been recalled during the 1908 Eucharistic Congress, when the plan to carry the Host through the streets of London had had to be abandoned.

At this stage the George Wise Protestant Crusade took a hand. George Wise was a tempestuous evangelist whose incendiary preaching attracted hundreds, and, in opinion and style, he personified a tradition of extreme Protestantism as old as the Reformation and still lively enough today. His inflamed view of Roman Catholicism as some kind of international conspiracy aimed at the overthrow of the British Constitution won him considerable support among those who liked their religion salty and red-blooded. Wise was one of several Protestants who registered their queries with the police. In a letter to Dunning, addressed from the Protestant Reformers' Memorial Church, he wrote:

> Kindly allow me to draw your special attention to the well-advertised Roman Catholic procession that is to take place in the neighbourhood of the Holy Cross, Great Crosshall Street, on Sunday afternoon next. It is believed that unless you interfere the priests will make an attempt to carry through the streets of the city the Host or consecrated wafer. This must never be allowed. Such is contrary to the laws of this country and is therefore absolutely illegal. I am writing to you solely in the interest of peace, and I shall be glad to have an assurance from you that no such attempt will be made.

Dunning felt able to reassure him and others, but in the meanwhile Burke found to his 'amazement' that the Health Committee had authorised the erection of an altar and assumed not unfairly that Dunning likewise had been informed. The Orangemen were satisfied by Dunning's assurance to the extent of cancelling a mass protest meeting.

L 177

The Holy Cross procession took place as planned. Ashton's report described it in the following terms:

> The vicar and churchwardens of St. Stephen's Protestant Church allowed a string of flags to be attached to their schools and other Protestants did the same for other buildings, or subscribed to the decorations fund. Among those who walked in the procession, about 4,500 in number, were members of the Italian colony, who carried on a litter borne on their shoulders a life-sized statue of the Madonna and Child, while at another point two small statues of the Saviour were carried by girls. When in the course of the procession the large statue passed the corner of Byrom Street and Dale Street —which are main thoroughfares—a few men began singing a Protestant hymn and made a rush for the statue. The mounted police came up, 'flanked' their horses on the crowd, and prevented any disturbance. There were no arrests and no further trouble occurred. The Chief Constable was in his office in uniform during the whole afternoon. There were some 250 police on the route of the procession, which lasted about an hour and a half. Mr. Caldwell, assistant head constable, reported to the Head Constable that two priests wore their cassocks and birettas in the procession. The questions which arise with reference to the legality of this procession will be dealt with at a later stage of this report. In connection with this jubilee 'altars' were put up in various courts in the district, which form one of the subjects against the police.

Almost immediately trouble began. The Health Committee and the police received a wide range of complaints from the Garston True Blues, the Star of Kirkdale Loyal Orange Lodge, the Protestant Labour Club, Joseph's Integrity Royal Black Preceptary and others. There was even a threat that repetition of such illegality would lead 'loyal Protestants' to 'take what steps we think proper to prevent it'. The Beresford Road Mission Hall Orange Lodge minced neither words nor opinions:

> 1. We consider it ill-advised on your part to permit Roman Catholic bands to desecrate the Sabbath day and annoy respectable citizens by the playing of the 'Boys of Wexford', etc., on the occasion of the Roman Catholic demonstration and procession, Sunday, May 9th, 1909.
> 2. Members of sodalities and confraternities paraded in monkish 'garb and girdle'; also a number of Acolytes, draped in the same emblematic dress as when serving Mass. . . . The Monks were expelled from England in 1579, 1581, 1586, 1602, and prevented from

entering in 1829; and now you will allow them to openly defy the law by parading our city and grant them police protection.

3. As the Roman Catholics are in a minority in Liverpool the above action means that the majority, who are Protestants, will have to bear the cost of extra duty for protecting an illegal procession.

4. The traffic was impeded and almost suspended on the route, several people nearly run over, and a tram inspector insulted and threatened for doing his duty. If no breach of the peace was suspected, why were the mounted police out? If you did suspect a breach, why was the procession allowed? We believe it is usual to stop anything which is calculated to cause a breach of the peace.

5. Religious emblems were carried. The stations of the cross promenaded, brass, wooden and floral crosses, in addition to two large painted and gilded chalk images and bannerette effigies of saints, etc., whilst the processionists sang 'Faith of our fathers', which is the supplicatory hymn to the Virgin to bring England back to popery. Should the ratepayers' money be spent in allowing and protecting this studied insult, in open disregard to all existing law? We respectfully submit that somebody has been fooling you. . . .

Very properly, especially in regard of an antiquated statute, Leonard Dunning asked the advice of the Home Office on this matter. He had now, of course, learned of the Health Committee's authorisation. He also reported fully to the Watch Committee, concluding with this sad and resigned appeal:

If the public highway were regarded and used for the sole purpose of going to and fro upon legitimate business and pleasure, Liverpool would enjoy a larger measure of peace than is possible when its streets are used, or rather abused, as places for the demonstration of adherence to this or abhorrence from that form of religious, political or social belief.

He sensed the forthcoming trouble likely to be caused by a clash of meetings on Sunday, 23 May, for the Catholic Young Men's Societies were to assemble at St George's Hall and the Orange Lodges a short distance away at Holy Trinity Church, St Anne Street. Both sides refused Dunning's request to postpone their meeting. The Roman Catholic Bishop, Thomas Whiteside, was most vigorous in his refusal to submit to 'a few noisy bigots', and 'a disreputable minority' who, he remembered feelingly, uttered 'their vile calumnies almost at my doors'. The day passed, however, without undue dislocation.

The Home Office and the Attorney-General were unhappily dilatory in advising the Chief Constable. It was 17 June, following three requests, that the Home Office saw fit to enunciate, and even then the advice was general and noncommittal, except on the very specific issue of carrying the Host. On the same day Dunning left for what he probably considered a well-earned holiday in—of all places—Ireland, and left the order of the city in charge of his assistant Mr Lane.

It was during the Head Constable's vacation that the contest, thus far a series of letters and meetings, boiled into violence. The occasion was a procession to mark the jubilee of St Joseph's (Grosvenor Street) Young Men's Society, complete with the Holy Cross Brass Band and a number of other colourful adjuncts. It was planned for 20 June 1909. The Grand Lodge of the Liverpool Province of the Orange Society reacted angrily. Despite Pastor Wise sounding a cautious note, a 'Monster Demonstration' was planned to be held in Juvenal Street an hour before the St Joseph's parade reached that point. It was advertised 'for the purpose of preventing any illegal processions'. 'Wake up, Protestant England!' was the message of the advertisement.

Lane made strenuous efforts to avoid an altercation. He persuaded the Catholics not to form a procession with statues, and the Protestant leaders to calm the fears of their adherents. 'If there is any of you who cannot behave yourselves, for goodness' sake stop away,' was in fact the final request of the Orange leadership to its members. Lane increased the police strength from 250 to 700 and again warned St Joseph's that the carriage of 'images or emblems' might lead to the termination of the parade. Unfortunately, the Catholics erected statues and altars at various points of the procession.

Sunday, 20 June, confirmed Lane's worst fears, and Ashton's report attempted to summarise a confused set of circumstances:

> From about 12.30 p.m. people began to assemble in Juvenal Street East, and about 2 o'clock the first encounter took place between the police and the crowd in that street. . . . While Juvenal Street East was being cleared by the police Mr. Lane turned to the Catholics, who were crowded behind the police at the east end of Juvenal Street West. . . . He then went to Prince Edwin Street and found there a general riot, in which the foot police could not hold their ground. He ordered two charges of the mounted police up

Prince Edwin Street and a cross charge along Beresford Street, which crosses Prince Edwin Street. At a quarter-past three he returned to St. Joseph's church and safely escorted the procession over the shortened route. The riot continued till late at night. One mounted policeman was knocked down with his horse, another policeman had his jaw broken, another was stabbed in the back. House windows were broken and one house was set on fire. By midnight Mr. Lane had a thousand men under his orders, and when he went home at two o'clock in the morning he left extra men on the streets for the rest of the night. Some forty or fifty persons were arrested, brought before the stipendiary magistrate on Monday morning, and remanded for a week.

During this week ending 26 June, outrages by one party upon the other occurred every night. Apart from crimes of violence, the Chief Constable's statistics show that the convictions for offences against property were on 20 June, 33; on 21 June, 23; on 2 June, 46; and on the last four days of the week 28 in all. Both the Protestant and the Catholic schools were closed. The constables were working watches of twelve instead of eight hours, and sixty of them were employed simply to guard property and persons.

Immediately Wise and others raised a clamour that the police were guilty of 'charging and battering the Orangemen about in a dastardly and cruel manner'. Grinning policemen had arrested 'respectable and orderly young men of excellent character', and led them through 'a howling, half-drunken Roman Catholic mob'. With a Mr Thomas as secretary, the Orange Order appointed a Defence Committee. Pastor Wise had thrown his earlier admirable caution to the winds, and preached on such themes as Jack the Ripper ('a Roman Catholic, as I believe he is') going to confession.

The Sunday following the St Joseph's procession was the date set by Pastor Wise for his Bible Class to take part in a procession in protest. But now Dunning took a firm stand. Wise having refused to abandon his procession, Dunning laid an information against him (Wise had a previous record of being ordered to keep the peace) and the magistrates issued a warrant for his arrest and also banned the proposed parade. Understandably, the Orangemen were furious. The papists had, they argued, enjoyed an illegal procession the previous week; now loyal Protestants were denied that privilege and their leader arrested. They further smarted the day after when four of their leading lights, together with forty-two others of both sects were haled before the courts to answer for their misdemeanours during the St Joseph's jubilee celebration. George Wise's case dragged on, with the Stipendiary Magistrate insisting on a recognisance of the pastor's good behaviour. The Protestant Bishop of Liverpool, about this time, joined with many of his clergy 'in condemning party processions'. The extreme Protestant wing, it will be seen, was rather isolated from the bosom of the established church.

The next stage involved Wise's refusal of the court's 'ordering him to enter into his own recognisances in the sum of £100 to keep the peace', and he was committed to a four-month prison term. It was then, in the August of 1909, that specific legal complaints about the erection of altars were laid, through solicitors, with the police and huge petitions and demonstrations called for an inquiry into police conduct. Feelings ran high and violence continued sporadically. Dunning remained the Orangemen's villain of the piece, while when their martyred hero George Wise returned to Walton jail after a vain appeal case, 100,000 supporters bid him a tumultuous farewell.

M. A. Maxwell, chairman of the Watch Committee, cleared the air a little by revealing that Dunning had had no say in the erection of the Marybone altar during the Holy Cross procession. This altar had become the symbol of the whole affair, and, said Maxwell, Dunning had been 'silently bearing the burden of a gross and unfounded allegation'. It was not, however, until the inquiry that the public learned that the Health Committee, in spite of Dunning's request, had not seen fit to reveal their part in the affair. The Health Committee's apparent diffidence about an officer, subject to another committee's jurisdiction, bearing the brunt of their mistake is one of the most unpleasant minor points connected with the case. However, by now the swell of feeling and the view that in any event an inquiry would resolve the whole discordant complex led to the Police (Liverpool Inquiry) Act being passed.

On examination the awesome array of accusations directed against the police fell apart at the seams. For instance, Superintendent Smith had purportedly led a wild, mounted baton charge shouting, 'Go for the bastards and give them hell.' On investigation the chief witness found he could not identify Smith, and in one way or another most of the charges began to appear as exaggerated or fabricated. Others, it became clear, were the result of complete misunderstandings or the consequence of inadequate memories of confused hours. There was little of certainty to be gleaned from what, in a flash of lyricism, Ashton called 'the dull background of incomplete recollection'. On the whole, Ashton exonerated the police from charges of brutality. One illustration of his treatment of specific complaints must suffice:

The next charge against the police under this head was made in connection with the rioting in Prince Edwin Street. The petitioners admitted that in Prince Edwin Street serious rioting broke out which continued for many hours, nor did they contend that the use of force there by the police was not justified. Their only complaint as to Prince Edwin Street consisted of two individual charges of violence against Inspector Foulkes. It was said that during the riots he struck two men brutally ... Mr. Thomas said that Inspector Foulkes struck down a young man at the corner of Iliad Street, who was simply standing as a spectator, and as he lay on the ground struck him about the legs. In cross-examination he said that there had been some stones thrown in the vicinity and the mounted police had just cleared the street. When the man was knocked down the crowd rushed at Foulkes and threw bricks at him, and if they had got hold of him would have used him brutally for his brutality ... another witness said she saw an inspector hit a man across the legs with his stick while he was on the ground. She did not know what the man was doing, but three policemen were hitting him and an inspector came and struck him over the legs. She saw this from the other side of the street.

Inspector Foulkes said he struck both the men. At Iliad Street a man called Prince threw a brick at the mounted police. He was arrested by a constable and they both fell. While on the ground Prince tried to kick and bite the constable. It was necessary to strike him to prevent the constable being maimed. Prince was afterwards fined at the police court. In Beresford Street the men had bars of iron, bricks for the men to throw from a back wall, which had been pulled down for the purpose. Someone struck Superintendent Tomlinson on the face with a missile, knocking his hat off. Someone picked up the hat, when a man came behind Tomlinson with half a brick saying, 'You bloody Dunning, I will brain you.' On this Inspector Foulkes knocked him down with his staff and was at once rushed across the street by the crowd, had to fight for his life and was rescued by other officers.

Edward Rishton, the constable who arrested Prince, said that Prince was trying to kick him in the stomach when Inspector Foulkes came up and that he himself was quite exhausted. This evidence was confirmed by Arthur Dukes, another constable, who arrested another man who was about to throw a large stone at Rishton. Superintendent Tomlinson confirmed the evidence of Inspector Foulkes with reference to Beresford Street, saying that he had been struck by missiles two or three times before the Inspector knocked the young man down.

Having seen Inspector Foulkes in the box, I had no difficulty in coming to the conclusion that the charge against him was unfounded. It seemed clear that if he had not done what he did he would have failed in his duty.

Apart from a slight predeliction to take police testimony at face value, A. J. Ashton does seem to have dealt justly with these complaints.

As for the by now famous Marybone altar, raised on a spot where St Patrick himself was said to have preached, the Orange representatives apologised handsomely to the Chief Constable once the full implications as to who had granted permission for its erection were explained and realised. The Roman Catholics pointed out the incontrovertible truth that it was not an 'altar' in a precise theological and sacramental sense and thus religious ceremonies could not be performed at it. There was a touch of sophistry here. The Catholic laity had erected this and other altars for years past and had not hesitated to practise forms of worship, even if these failed to meet the more rigorous canons of their church. It was possibly expecting a little too much of the opposition faction that they would appreciate such subtle distinctions. Dunning had again suffered in this case through the Protestants' failure to comprehend that, if the Head Constable, 'informed' the Attorney-General (as of course he did) prosecution would automatically follow. The Orangemen assumed Dunning had not considered such a step.

In the event several charges referring to police 'preferential treatment' of Catholics were withdrawn. To his credit, George Wise spoke up manfully:

> The revelations in this court, made during the examination of all the witnesses, particularly concerning Mr. Dunning, have wonderfully impressed me, and up to that moment I regarded Mr. Dunning

as terribly biassed against me. I regarded him as one that harassed me very much, and more than that I regarded him and Mr. Tomlinson, and others, as men who went out of their way to prevent me having the liberty of the subject so far as the processions and public meetings were concerned. But it is very evident from the revelations made here, there have been misunderstandings, misjudgements, and to a very large degree undue exaggerations. I would like to leave the matter there, and I believe, honestly believe, that counsel, I do not mean counsel in the ordinary legal sense of the word, but confidence, on all these matters, so far as the future is concerned, would tend to the better government of the city.

Lastly, the commissioner turned to the background to the disturbances, beginning with an unexceptional statement to the effect that:

> The predisposing cause of these disturbances is to be found in the fact that Roman Catholics and Protestants living in neighbouring districts, which imperceptibly shade into one another, are alike animated and at times dominated, by intense sectarian feeling. In these districts to sing 'The Boys of Wexford' on the one hand or 'The Boyne Water' or 'Derry Walls' on the other hand is no light matter. St. Patrick's Day and Orangemen's Day always yield some trouble. And indeed where the same external circumstances express to one man in very truth the presence of his God and to his neighbour the idolatry of perishable matter, and where conviction is in each case saturated with feeling, slight causes may produce far-reaching results. If the seed of strife is sown in such soil it yields abundantly the evil fruits of crime, oppression and misery.

From this he traced the development of the varied disturbances, pointing out how, in an inflammatory atmosphere, fact and appearance differ. He cited the dress and emblems of the Roman Catholic processions, observing that these could give to the lay observer a marked impression of illegality. He went on to demonstrate the possible results of sectarian strife, mentioning the case of William Daniels.

> He worked at a mill where 75 per cent of the men were Roman Catholics. Immediately after the Holy Cross procession he had taken to the mill and sharpened there the sword which he had with him in Juvenal Street East on June 20th. On June 21st he went to his work as usual at 6.30 a.m. and went in by a side entrance. At breakfast time an angry crowd of Roman Catholics had gathered

outside and the foreman kept him in the mill; later in the day the crowd threatened to burn the mill unless Daniels was put out, and six policemen were brought to escort him away. In spite of his escort he was hit over the head with a pair of tongs by a woman who got six weeks' imprisonment for the attack. He had been at this mill seventeen years and had never had any trouble with his fellow workmen before, but after June 20th he was never able to return to this mill and was out of work altogether for six weeks.

He also attacked the provocative marches of Orange bands, particularly the 'scratch bands' some of which were not official Orange troupes, and he unequivocally condemned George Wise and the George Wise Crusade as being a major cause of the disturbances under review. He obtained from Wise a firm promise to temper his commentaries on Roman Catholic doctrine in the future.

In closing his report Arthur Ashton made the following point:

> So far as the public streets and highways are concerned, processions and meetings stand on the same footing. A meeting is a procession at rest and a procession is a meeting in motion. The special circumstances of this district of Liverpool are admittedly peculiar. I think there was a feeling among those who came before me, not confined to any one party, that the hands of those responsible for the order of the city might well be strengthened. I have already suggested the possibility of a Conciliation Board, which could advise on questions concerning ceremonies and ritual. Perhaps I may be allowed to apply to Parliament for powers under which religious processions and religious meetings in open unenclosed spaces should be allowed only when they had been previously sanctioned by the authorities, whether by the Lord Mayor in writing upon petition presented, or by other suitable means. Such a measure would enable limitations to be put upon the number of processions, their route, and their constitution, and upon the manner in which open-air meetings are conducted: by appropriate provisions it might give the executive less clumsy methods than the ordinary law affords of preventing meetings or processions altogether.

So a rather petty and rather messy episode ended. It epitomised religious strife and delineated it in minature. Like a kind of theological *Animal Farm*, it is possible to see the characters involved as analogical puppets playing the roles of grander and more tempestuous contests ranging from the sixteenth to the twentieth century. Perhaps the persons themselves had a conscious inkling of this. Perhaps Pastor Wise especially saw himself in a twin reincarnation of Martin Luther and William III. Since 1897 his campaign against ritualism in the established church and against what he saw as the physical and spiritual threat of Rome, coupled with his 'remarkably successful' temperance work, had won him a huge support which he held 'in the hollow of his hand'. His Bible class alone numbered 1,600. The Catholics regarded him with deep hatred and enmity and, according to Ashton, their counter-accusations were over-exaggerated. Poor Leonard Dunning was caught in the crossfire and suffered what he called 'living for months in a hell on earth'. His burden was that of the administrator, faced with the problem of passively bearing an undeserved blame. The explosive mixture was there; the flashpoint, as unnecessary and trivial as flashpoints so often are with these events, lay in the minutes of the city's Health Committee. They sanctioned an altar without having the authority and later failed to clarify the point in Dunning's favour.

Bibliography

There may be those who found this set of sketches either so frustrating or, more optimistically, so stimulating that they wish to turn to a more substantial consideration of Liverpool. The primary and the secondary sources alike are inexhaustible and the Liverpool Public Record Office and Local History Library at the Picton Reference Library is as pleasingly and helpfully stocked and organised as any in the country. It is usually agreed that no definitive volume on the history of Liverpool has been published, but some approach this elusive mark of approbation, viz, G. Chandler, *Liverpool*; F. A. Bailey, *The Story of Liverpool*; J. Touzeau, *Rise and Progress of Liverpool 1551–1835*; Ramsey Muir, *A History of Liverpool*. A recent publication of twenty-four talks given on Radio Merseyside must be heartily recommended as an uncomplicated clear-cut and attractive introduction; this is J. J. Bagley, *The Story of Merseyside*, Part One (1968) and Part Two (1969). B. D. White, *A History of the Corporation of Liverpool* (1951), is another certain stand-by for the student of Liverpool's social, administrative, and political development.

Specialist topics often have first-rate coverage; for example, E. Broxap, *The Great Civil War in Lancashire*, and G. Chandler and E. K. Wilson, *Liverpool under Charles I*, deal with the Civil War period effectively; C. N. Parkinson, *The Rise of the Port of Liverpool*, and A. S. Mountfield, *Western Gateway: A History of the Mersey Docks and Harbour Board*, trace the development of Liverpool as a port with sure competence; while G. S. Veitch, *The Struggle for the Liverpool and Manchester Railway* offers a readable account of the major breakthrough in overland transportation.

There are any number of contemporary sources like the Blundell diaries, Picton's *Memorials of Liverpool* and Ellen Weeton's journals, and there are a considerable number of sound biographies, like G. Chandler's *William Roscoe of Liverpool 1753-1831.* One can turn to a voluminous collection of manuscript, municipal, directory and newspaper sources, while the *Victoria County History* and the *Transactions of the Lancashire and Cheshire Historic Society* and the *Transactions of the Lancashire and Cheshire Antiquarian Society* may also be consulted.

Turning to the specific essays assembled here, the available reading is as inconsistent as the choice of topics. Some guidance might be found in the following list.

Chapter One. *The Theatre Royal and after.* There is no specialist work on the Theatre Royal itself. For any student of Liverpool theatre history R. J. Broadbent, *Annals of the Liverpool Stage* (1908), is the most careful and voluminous guide, while the *Liverpool Theatrical Investigator* is a valuable journal for the early years of Merseyside theatre. Newspaper reviews and the many theatre programmes kept in the Picton Library are additional sources.

Chapter Two. *The first Grand National.* Again, newspapers are by far the best approach to the Grand National and most of the histories do little more than draw on these, in particular the racing press. However, J. Formby, *An Account of the Liverpool Races* (1828) throws fascinating light on the early controversy. C. O'Leary, *Grand National* (1947) and V. Smith, *Grand National* (1969) are possibly the clearest modern narrative accounts.

Chapter Three. *The inauguration of the Liverpool Police Force.* Amazingly, there is no worthwhile account of Liverpool police history in its opening stages. Conversely, the primary sources are very strong. The Liverpool Watch Committee Minutes and the Chief Constable's Annual Reports (1836 on) are the basis of these, but there are many other accounts, both municipal and independent, of the activities of the police and of the opening and operating of Walton Prison.

Chapter Four. *Liverpool and the new Poor Law.* The most lucid rehearsal of Liverpool's unusual relation with the new Poor Law is the government's own report, viz. 1842 Parlty. Papers: *Grounds of Exemption for Liverpool from Poor Law Amendment Act*, XXV (232). For a hindsight view of the new régime W. Rathbone, *Local Taxation and Poor Law Administration in Great Cities—Liver-*

Bibliography

pool (1869), presents the interesting case of a well-known Liverpolitan figure. W. L. Blease, 'The Old Poor Law', *Lancs. and Ches. Antiq. Soc.* (1909), describes the old Poor Law for those anxious to obtain a before-and-after image.

Chapter Five. *The cholera and Doctor Duncan.* Unlike police work and education, the amount of material available in the fields of public health, sanitation, water-supply and medicine is quite staggering. Two or three 'starters' only can be mentioned: W. H. Duncan, *Medical Officer of Health for Liverpool, Annual Reports* (1847–62); W. M. Frazer, *Duncan of Liverpool* (1947); and T. A. Bickerton, *A Medical History of Liverpool* (1920).

Chapter Six. *The struggle for water and drains.* J. Newlands, *Liverpool Past and Present in relation to Sanitary Operations* (1859); E. W. Hope, *Evolution of Sanitation in Liverpool* (1896); and G. H. Pumphrey, *Liverpool's Public Services* (1900) are three of many choices.

Chapter Seven. *The early years of the Liverpool School Board.* The very full volumes of the Liverpool School Board, Minutes and Reports (1871–1902), give a much more substantial account than, for instance, the Education Committee minutes of this century. It is just as well, for little or no definitive writing has been done in this field. As with law and order and public health, some of the Liverpool periodicals, notably *Porcupine*, are of value in the educational field. One might especially mention that interesting series of articles by 'A Liverpool Shipwright'; 'Education, Past and Present', in *Porcupine* (1877).

Chapter Eight. *Everton Football Club: the opening seasons.* Once more the press is an indispensable ally, but two books stand out to assist the football researcher. The first is T. Delaney, *A Century of Soccer* (1963), a fine background work, published on the centenary of the Football Association. The second is P. M. Young, *Football on Merseyside* (1963), one of Young's several closely-argued, readable but never mundane recitals of football club histories.

Chapter Nine. *The retail revolution: David Lewis and Owen Owen.* Business history is a newer branch of the profession. Luckily, apart from obvious press and store records, both men have been treated bibliographically in vastly divergent but highly useful styles. A. Briggs, *Friends of the People* (1957), is the history of Lewis's by a master historian. Needless to say, it is a model of its kind. I. Hargreaves, *They Always Come Back* (1968), is the official centenary history of Owen Owens, but it is not lacking in analysis and comments.

Chapter Ten. *The fame of Florence Maybrick.* Thousands of words have been spilled over this most written-about case. The four most helpful works are: T. L. Christie. *Etched in Arsenic* (1969), the latest and most broad-ranging, H. B. Irving, *Trial of Mrs Maybrick* (1912), is an annotated transcript of the trial, F. E. Maybrick, *Mrs Maybrick's Own Story* (1904), the lady's own somewhat roseate justification and N. Morland, *This Friendless Lady* (1957), is an elegantly written commentary.

Chapter Eleven. *The sectarian troubles and the Police Inquiry of 1909–10.* No direct book nor article has been written on this topic. An enormously detailed blow-by-blow recital is provided by the lengthy *Proceedings of the 1909 Liverpool Police Inquiry Act* (1910). L. Dunning, Head Constable's Annual Report (1910), and a rather hagiographical book, R. F. Henderson, *George Wise of Liverpool* (1911), offer varying slants on this sad episode.

It has been suggested that newspapers form one of the liveliest sources for many of these topics. The major ones to consult would be the *Liverpool Mercury*, a Whig-cum-Liberal daily, and the *Liverpool Courier*, its Tory equivalent. For later years the *Liverpool Daily Post*, founded in 1855, and its evening stable companion, the *Liverpool Echo*, are the newspapers to consider.

The study of Liverpool's late history is diverting and important. In spite of some strange gaps, there are materials aplenty for the willing researcher. What is lacking is a good range of monographs on so many of these significant themes. Some topics have been hammered remorselessly, but there are dozens awaiting serious treatment. There are businesses, organisations, particularly recreational and religious ones, notable individuals, like Whittle, Bushell, or Newlands, institutions, such as the workhouse or the hospitals and several interesting events, like the great Liverpool hurricane or the 'Alabama' incident which are either obscurely described in academic journals or not at all. There is a wealth of sources to match the wealth of possibilities, yet Liverpool by comparison, say, with Manchester has too few pleasing and competent accounts of its own historical progress. There could be a hundred *Old Liverpool*s without the need for repetition. Such has been the spicy variety of life in this unfathomable city, complex alike in character, growth and attitude.

Acknowledgements

Illustrations form an integral element of this book. I am deeply indebted to Terry Mulrooney and Raymond Farley for their diligence and skill in tracking down some illustrations and producing others; they took on the task of conjuring up the illustrative material cheerfully and efficiently and I am most warmly grateful to them.

Particular pictures require particular acknowledgement. The Liverpool Corporation City Engineer's Department (Photo Section) kindly permitted me to use the photograph of Chatsworth School, Everton FC allowed me the use of their two team photographs and Lewis's Ltd and Owen Owen Ltd gave me permission to publish the photographs of their stores. I would like to thank the Picton Library, Liverpool, for their assistance in providing facilities for Raymond Farley and Terry Mulrooney to reproduce all the other illustrations, except for those of the converted Theatre Royal, the Empire Theatre, Walton Prison and the Leighton Dene Old People's Home, which Raymond Farley photographed independently.

I am also most grateful to Miss M. Byrne for performing the laborious task of preparing the typescript with such skill and competence.

ERIC MIDWINTER

Index

Plates are indicated in bold.

Accrington, 86
Addison, Mr, 166
Adelphi, 34
Aickin, F., 26
Aigburth, 16, 22, 169
Aintree, 40–50
Akbar Reformatory, 59
Albert St, 110
Alcock, C. W., 137, 138
'A Liverpool Shipwright', 124–9
Allerton, 22
American Slave Serenades, 31
Amphitheatre, 23, 32, 34
Anfield, 21
Anfield Road, 136, 140, 148
Anglican Cathedral, 21, 174
Argyll Theatre, 37
Arnold, A., 131
Ashfield Street School, 123
Ashton, A. J., 174–87
Askey, Arthur, 24
Aspinall, A., 75, 76
Audley House, 156, 158
Aughton, 41

Bachelor, Mr, 59, 60
Bainbridge, G., 34
Bala, Lake, 104
Ball, A., 145, 174
Banner, H., 103
Barnum, S., 154
Bargery, G., 135
Basnett Street, 156
Battlecrease House, 169–70
Baxter, Dr J. C., 140
Beatles, The, 23, 24
Beaufort Street School, 123
Becher, Captain, 45, 50
Bedford, Duchess of, 165
Bennett, Mrs, 25

Bennett, W., 104–5
Bentinck, Lord George, 49, 51, 52
Beresford Road Mission Hall, 178–9
Beresford Street, 183–4
Bermuda, 57
Bickerton, T. H., 93
Birkenhead, 14, 37
Birkenhead, Lord, 170
Birmingham, 156
Blackburn, 43, 86
Blaug, M., 73
Blease, W. L., 67
Blundells, the, 172–3
Boardman, J., 75
Bolton, 81, 174
Booth, C., 173
Booth, H., 67, 68
Bon Marche, 150, 156
Bootle, 13, 14, 15, 16
Bootle FC, 133, 134
Bootle Water Co, 101–3
Boucicant, A., 150, 156
Bourne, S., 67, 69
Boylett, A., 137
Bretherton, B., 50
Brettle, F., 137
Brierley, A., 162, 164
Briggs, A., 149
British Medical Journal, 98
Broadbent, R. J., 39
Brougham, Lord, 124
Brownlow Hill, 15, 80
Brunswick Street, 25
Bryden, Mr, 75
Bryant, A., 42
Bunbury, Sir C., 43
Burke, Councillor, 176, 177
Burke & Hare, 93
Burke, T., 97
Bushell, C., **90**, 116, 127

Index

Butler Street School, 123

Cadburys, 152
Caldwell, Asst Chief Constable, 178
Cambridge University, 131, 132, 133
Campbell, Rev A., 75, 79
Campbell, Mr, 132
Canning Place, 13
Castle Street, 14
Case, G., 26
Caton, 74
Celeste, Madame, 31
Chadwick, Mr, 139, 145
Chadwick, Sir E., 62, 63, 65, 68, 76, 91, 103, 109
Chambers, W., 25
Chandler, W., 162
Chapel Street, 14
Chartres Street, 25, 102
Chatham Street, 20
Chatsworth Street School, 20, 107, 123
Chester, 13, 14
Cholera, 73, 85, 99, 101, 111
Chorley, 104, 105,
Clarence Street, 157
Clarke, D., 37
Clarke, J. W., 134
Clay, J., 55
Clayton Square, 158
Clayton, W. R., 140
Clint Road School, 123
Cockpit Yard Theatre, 24
Cohen, G., 158
Cohen, L., 157
Coleman, T., 43, 48
Collins, W., 171
Colter, A. B., 176
Constabulary Commission, 55-9, 62
Cooper, Councillor, 96
Cooke, G. F., 29
Covent Garden, 26
Cribb, T., 131
Crosbie, S., 137
Crosby, 15, 43
Cromwell, D., 132, 173
Crown Street, 21-2
Croxteth, 13, 22
Cruitt's Field, Priory Road, 136
Cuff, W. C., 133

Dale Street, 14
Daniels, W., 185-6
Darwin, C., 133

Davies, J., 66
Dean, Dixie, 145
Derby, Earl of, 34, 48, 61, 160
Dick, A., 138
Dickens, C., 31
Dobson, G., 138
Dock Committee, 14
Dodd, Ken, 24
Dooley, A., 21
Dowling, Supt, 62, 63
Drake, Charlie, 37
Drury Lane, 26
Drury Lane Theatre, 25
Dublin, 70
Duncan, Dr, 12, 85-99, 89
Dunning, L., 176-87

Eckersley, J., 75, 76, 77
Edge Hill, 15, 61
Edinburgh University, 91, 94
Education Act, 1870, 115-23
Edwards, J., 60
Eglington, Earl of, 48
Egremont, Lord, 43
Elmore, J., 50
Empire Theatre, 31-8, 36
Erskine, Lord, 47
Evans, Councillor, 96
Evans, J., 75, 79
Everton, 16, 61
Everton Brow, 15, 19
Everton FC, 12, 108, 125, 131-48
Everton Heights, 15
Exchange Station, 19
Exchange Street East, 62

Farmer, G., 138
Farr, W., 88
Farrer, E., 26, 27
Faulkner Square, 157
Flanagan, Mrs, 169, 170
Flint, E., 118
Ford, E., 79
Formby, J., 43, 45, 48
Forster, W. E., 115, 122, 123
Foster, Mr, 28
Foster, W., 79
Foulkes, Insp, 183-4

Garrick, D., 26, 31
Garstang, 81
Garston, 22

Index

Geary, F., 139
General Board of Health, 95
Gibson, Mr, 24, 26
Gilbert & Sullivan, 30, 33, 34
Gladstone Docks, 14
Gladstone, H., 174
Gladstone, W. E., 11, 15, 20, 83, 91, 115, 174
Goodison Park, 20, 140, 141, 142, 145, 146, 148
Granby, 16
Granby Street, 20
Grand National, 12, 40-52, 53, 162
Grand Theatre, 38
Gray, E., 75, 79
Great Eastern, the, 154
Great George's Place, 20
Great Howard Street, 66
Greg, S., 121
Greig, Major, 116
Greenbow, E. H., 88
Grey, Lord, 51
Grimaldi, J., 29-30
Gwladys Street, 146
Gwynne, Nell, 24

Hackins Hey, 19
Haly Price Riots, 30
Halton, J. P., 95
Handley, Tommy, 24
Hardy, S., 142
Harrington, 16
Harrington School, 123
Harrod, A. C., 150, 151
Hart, C., 24
Hartley, J., 14
Hawthorne, Dr, 96
Hawsley, T., 104
Hazlitt, W., 42
Health of Towns Advocate, 94
Henderson, G., 69-73
Higgins, Mrs, 169, 170
High Street, 14
Hill, R., 129
Holme, S., 88, 103
Holmes, J., 61
Holt, G., 105
Holt, J., 139
Holy Cross Church, 175, 176, 182
Hope Street, 21, 174
Houghton, R., 79
Houlding, J., 137-41
Hoylake, 40

Hughes, Mr, 163, 164, 171
Hughes, T., 133
Hughes, T. J., 158
Hume, A., 80-1
Hunter, A., 139
Huskisson, W., 21
Hyam's of Lord Street, 152

Irish, the, 11, 70, 76, 81-2, 95-7, 172, 173, 180
Irving, H., 31-2, 38
Isle of Man, 83
Islington, 13

Jacobs, Mr, 153
Jameson, W., 66
James Street Station, 19
Jeffery, J. R., 104-5
Juggler Street, 24

Kear, C., 29
Kean, E., 29
Kemble, F., 29
Kemble, J., 27, 29
Kensington, 16
Kirkby, 19
Kirkdale, 16, 22, 58, 61, 84, 169
King, Hetty, 38
Kingsley, C., 133
Kinnaird, Lord A., 133, 141, 142
Knight, Mr, 28
Knowsley Hall, 24
Knox, Dr, 93
Koch, 94

Lace Street, 96
Lancashire, 12, 23, 44, 69, 73, 74, 81-3, 85, 86, 88, 91
Lancaster, 74, 85
Lane, Asst Chief Constable, 180-1
L'Angelier, 169
Lata, 139, 148
Latham House, 24
Lawrence, H., 75
Leather Lane, 19
Lee, G. H., 156
Leigh, 40
Leno, D., 34
Levy, B., 158
Levy, M., 157
Levy, W., 153
Lewis, B. (*née* Coten), 156-7
Lewis, D. (Lewis's), 12, 19, **126**, 149-60
Lewis, Mr, 28

Index

Lewis, T. F., 74
Lime Street, 15, 16
Lime Street Station, 16, 92
Little Crosby, 173
Liverpool Board of Health, 92
Liverpool City Council, 115
Liverpool College of Building, 20
Liverpool Collegiate, 20
Liverpool Courier, 49, 73, 157
Liverpool Cricket Club, 169
Liverpool Daily Albion, 157, 160
Liverpool Daily Post, 98
Liverpool Dispensaries, 91
Liverpool Education Committee, 117, 130
Liverpool FC, 131, 136, 141, 142
Liverpool Fever Hospitals, 73, 92–4
Liverpool Guardian Society, 101
Liverpool Harrington Water Company, 101–3
Liverpool Health Committee, 95–9, 103, 110–13, 176–87
Liverpool Highways Board, 101–3, 109, 110
Liverpool Houseowners' Association, 113, 119–20
Liverpool International Exhibition, 154
Liverpool Journal, 57
Liverpool–Leeds Canal, 15, 42, 52, 149
Liverpool–Leeds Railway, 11, 15, 149
Liverpool Mail, 63
Liverpool Medical Gazette, 92–4
Liverpool Medical Institutes, 94
Liverpool Medical Relief Committee, 96
Liverpool Mercury, 50, 63, 64, 65, 73, 74, 75, 92, 93, 96, 103, 106
Liverpool Nuisance Department, 112–13
Liverpool Police Force, 61–6
Liverpool Police Inquiry, 109, 110, 172–87
Liverpool Police Strike, 58
Liverpool poor law, 67–84
Liverpool Poor Law Act, 78, 79
Liverpool Poor Law Guardians, 75–80
Liverpool Sanitary Act, 95, 96, 103, 110
Liverpool School Board, 115–30
Liverpool Select Vestry, 67–81
Liverpool Standard, 46
Liverpool Theatrical Advertiser, 30
Liverpool University, 20
Liverpool Workhouse, 61, 69–71, 83, 84
Liver Theatre, 31
Lloyd, Marie, 38

Lockhead, 139
London, 13, 56, 120, 152, 175, 177
London Road, 153
Lowe, J., 135
Low Hill, 61, 62
Lunesdale, 74
Luther, M., 187
Lynn, W., 44–52
Lyric, 38
Lythgoe, R. E., 133, 134, 138

Macklin, C., 26
Maclaren, A. C., 132
Macready, W. C., 26
Maghull, 43–6
Mahon, G., 140
Makepeace, H., 145
Manchester, 11, 12, 15, 26, 34, 67, 74, 78, 85, 92, 109, 111, 141, 149, 152, 155
Marks and Spencer, 149, 158
Marriot, T., 135
Martin, 'Humanity', 47
Marybone Altar, the, 176–87
Mason, J., 50
Matthews, C., 28
Mattocks, G., 25, 26
Maxwell, M. A., 182
Maybrick, E., 163, 164
Maybrick, Mrs. F., 12, 144, 161, 171
Maybrick, G., 163
Maybrick, J., 162
Maybrick Jnr, 163
Maybrick, M., 163, 164
McDonough, A., 46, 47, 49–50
McFarlane, 139
McGill, J., 135, 148
McGregor, W., 138
McKenna, J., 141
McKinley, President, 165
Mellon, H., 27
Mellor, J., 79
Melville, H., 82
Mersey Docks & Harbour Board, 14
Mersey River, 13, 14, 16, 40, 149, 151, 154, 155, 157
Mersey Tunnel, 15
Metropolitan Cathedral, 21, 174
Metropolitan Police, 61, 63, 65
Milward, 139, 141, 145, 148
Molyneux, Lord, 43–6
Monthly Mirror, 27, 28
Moor Street, 24
Moore, Carrie, 38

Index

Morecambe and Wise, 38
Morris, B., 135
Moss Empires, 37
Mott, C., 76–8
Mount Pleasant, 15, 20
Mount Vernon, 15
Muir, R., 67
Murphy, F., 57

Nassau Senior, 68
Netherleigh, 19
Newlands, J., 110–14
Newsham Park, 16
New South Wales, 57
North Corporation Street School, 20, 115, 120
Norman, D., 158

Old Etonians, 133
Oldhall Street, 14
Old Harrovians, 132, 133
Oliver, T., 51
Orange Lodges, 124, 172–86
Ormskirk, 20, 41
Orrell's Brewery Field, 136
Our Lady's Church, Everton, 133
Owen, D., 158
Owen, Owen, 19, 143, 149–60
Owen, S., 152
Oxford University, 131, 132, 133

Paganini, 30
Palmer, Mr, 27
Parkinson, P., 137
Parlow, Supt, 61
Peel, Sir R., 59, 76, 78, 177
Pentonville, 66
Pierhead, 15, 19
Pit, the, 175
Playfair, L., 87–8
Pooley, H., 121
Poal, the, 13, 14
Poor Law Commission, 73–81, 87
Porcupine, the, 124–9
Potts, H., 46
Powell, A., 51
Power, A., 74, 76, 78
Prescot, 15
Preston, 15, 42, 55, 57, 82, 86, 173
Prince Edwin Street, 180–4
Prince Edwin Street School, 137
Prince Rupert, 19, 24, 132
Princes Avenue, 21

Princes Park, 16, 19, 157
Privy Council Department of Education 115–24
Provan, 135, 148

Queens Drive, 16
Queens Road School, 20, 123, 127, 128
Queens Theatre, 38

Ranelagh Street, 153
Rathbone, S. F., 121, 123, 173
Rathbone, W., 83, 84, 103, 111, 121, 173
Ray, Ted, 24
Richards, E., 157
Rivington Pike, 104–6, 112, 113
Robertson, J. D., 140
Robey, G., 37
Robson, E. R., 120
Rodney Street, 20, 91
Roscoe, Dr, 67
Roscommon Street, 123
Ross, N., 139
Rotunda, 38
Rous, Admiral, 48
Rowal, Col, 61
Rowlands, Mr, 75
Royal Alexandra Theatre, 31
Royal Birkdale Golf Club, 40
Royal Court Theatre, 23, 34, 37, 38
Royal Liverpool Golf Club, 40
Royal Poor Law Commission, 69–70
Royal, J., 145
Runcorn, 19
Russell, Lord J., 124, 127
Russell, Sir C., 165–7

Sandon Hotel, 137, 138
Sanitary Amendment Act, 11
Salford, 70, 82, 85
Scotland Road, 16, 20, 96
Scott, E., 142, 145
Sefton, Earl of, 44, 48, 57
Sefton Park, 16
Shakespeare Theatre, 34, 38
Shakespeare, W., 24, 33
Sharp, J., 142–3
Shaw Street, 20, 62
Sheil Park, 16
Shimmins, H., 65, 66
Shipp, J., 61
Sir Thomas Street, 20
Siddons, J., 26, 27
Siddons, S., 26, 27
Simon, Sir John, 88, 91

Index

Sims, G. R., 83
Sirdefield, W., 46
Skelmersdale, 13, 19
Smith, M., 169, 171
Smith's Liverpool Weekly, 38
Smith, Supt, 182–3
Smith, T., 174
Snow, 94
Soho Street, 20
South Coporation School, 115, 120
Southport, 15, 20, 172
Speke, 19
Spencer Court, 87
Sprigg, T., 131
Squires, W. W., 93, 94
St Albans, 43, 46, 49
St Benedict's Church, 133
St Domingo's Vale Church, 131–3, 137
St George's Hall, 166, 167
St Helens, 40, 57, 173
St John's Church, Bootle, 133
St Peter's Church, 133, 147
Stanley, Lord, 48
Stanley Park, 16, 134, 136
Stanley Parkists, 134
Star, 38
Stephen, Mr Justice, 164, 165, 166
Stephenson, R., 105
Stratton, Eugene, 38
Sudell, Major W., 137
Suter, F., 135

Tate, Harry, 37
Tattersalls, 42
Theatre Royal, 12, 23–34, 35, 39, 61
Thomas, Mr, 181, 183
Thring, F. C., 132
Tilley, V., 37
Times, The, 167
Tinne, J. A., 111
Tithebarn Street, 14, 163
Topham, E. W., 51, 52
Tomlinson, Supt, 183–4
Toxteth Park, 13, 16, 22, 57, 61, 92
Tree, E., 29
Trench, W. S., 98
Trevelyan, G. O., 148
Turner, F. J., 23
Tussaud's Waxworks, 167, 168
Tyldesley, J. T., 132
Tweedley, Tommy, 37

Union Court, 87

United Church Club, 134
Upper Park Street School, 123
Uppingham School, 132

Vandenhoff, J., 28, 29
Vauxhall Road, 65, 91, 92, 96
Victoria, Queen, 160, 165
Von Roques, Baron, 162–3
Von Roques, Baronness, 162–3, 165

Wade, A. R., 133
Wainwright, T., 166
Wallace, J., 161
Wallace, W., 161, 166, 171
Walton Gaol, 54, 66, 162
Walton Lane School, 123,
Walton Park, 16
Wanamaker, J., 150
Wanderers, the, 133
Warrington, 15, 40, 82, 85, 106, 173
Water Street, 14, 15, 19, 24, 62
Waverton Park, 16
Wavertree, 22
Wayne, R., 63
Weatherby's, 42
Wellington, Duke of, 177
Welsh Charity School, 120, 173
West Derby, 13, 22
Whitechapel, 13, 25
Whiteside, Bishop T., 179
Whiteley, W., 150
Whitworth, 111
Whitty, M. J., 54, 63
Wigan, 13, 40, 85
Wilkinson, C., 21, 103
Wilkinson, J., 79
William III, 172, 174, 187
William Brown Street, 19
Williamson Square, 25, 30, 56
Wilton, Earl of, 48
Wilton, Robb, 24
Wirral, The, 15, 16, 19, 56
Wise, G., 144, 175–87
Wise, G., Crusade, 175–87
Wood, J. R., 87
Woodford, Sir J., 65, 66
Woolton, 22, 102
Woolwich, 58, 59
Woolworth, F. W., 151

Yapp, A., 163, 164, 171
York, 63
Young, A., 135
Younger, J., 25, 26, 27